INDEPENDENCE MEMORIES

To the 69ers – childhood friends in Muckross Park,
who grew into kind, adventurous young women,
travelled the earth, mothered a generation,
changed the world, loved and laughed.
Wise women, all.

VALERIE COX

INDEPENDENCE MEMORIES

A People's Portrait of the
Early Days of the Irish Nation

HACHETTE
BOOKS
IRELAND

First published in Ireland in 2021 by HACHETTE BOOKS IRELAND
First published in paperback in 2022

A CIP catalogue record for this book is available from
the British Library.

ISBN 978 1 52933 985 7

Typeset in Sabon LT Std by Bookends Publishing Services, Dublin
Printed and bound in Great Britain by Clays Ltd, Elcograf, S.p.A.

Front cover image: A young girl peeps around as the Blessed Sacrament
passes along a street in Cork. The procession was part of the centenary
celebrations for Catholic Emancipation, July 1929.

Hachette Books Ireland policy is to use papers that are
natural, renewable and recyclable products and made
from wood grown in sustainable forests. The logging and
manufacturing processes are expected to conform to the
environmental regulations of the country of origin.

Hachette Books Ireland
8 Castlecourt Centre
Castleknock
Dublin 15, Ireland

A division of Hachette UK Ltd
Carmelite House, 50 Victoria Embankment, EC4Y 0DZ

www.hachettebooksireland.ie

CONTENTS

Introduction

The Irish War of Independence and the subsequent Civil War made Ireland a turbulent and dangerous place to live, the former lasting from 21 January 1919 to 11 July 1921 and the latter from 28 June 1922 to 24 May 1923. Our collective memories are still raw, stories have been handed down through generations of the raids carried out by the Black and Tans, of the women who were runners for Michael Collins, bullets carefully sewn into the hems of their skirts. Colette Cox tells me the story of her mother, Eileen Scanlon: 'This is how it worked – somebody would write the smallest amount of information on a piece of paper, as small as a stamp, and her mother would do her long hair for her, up in a bun, and she would hide the piece of paper in the bun.'

Then there was the tragedy of those who lost their lives in the conflicts. It is estimated that between 300 and 400 civilians were killed during the Civil War, some of them tragic bystanders like 19-year-old Mary Ellen Kavanagh, shot dead during a bank raid in Buncrana in 1922. The family was offered compensation of 19 pounds, one pound for every year of her life.

Collecting those memories during Covid was a strange experience. There was no chatting over cups of tea or settling in at a cosy fire, no hugs or handshakes with new friends. We couldn't walk the land where these incidents took place or visit the cottages, thatch collapsed and open to the rain, where ambushes were plotted and people went on the run, the safe houses with their secret rooms and large cupboards. Instead our interviews were conducted by phone or Zoom calls, the sterility of it the complete opposite of the stories, the colour, the life-affirming efforts of a people determined to survive.

But against this background of armies and rebels and brothers divided by civil war, people got on with their lives. They walked to school and fell in love, raised their families and worked their farms. They laid their dead to rest and dreamed and built the foundations of a future Ireland.

It's been over a century so these are family memories, of parents, grandparents and even earlier generations. But there is one exception, 107-year-old Máirín Hughes who remembers being in the Mercy convent in Killarney in 1922 when there was an attack on the RIC barracks up the road. The nuns gave the children milk and sandwiches and kept them in school for safety's sake until 5 p.m. Máirín was eight years old at the time and I've included her amazing story here. It was such a privilege to chat to someone who was actually an eyewitness.

These stories also include the 200,000 Irishmen who left home to join the British army and who fought in the First World War. My own grandfather, Terence FitzPatrick, was a territorial soldier in the army service corps. He fought at the Battle of the Somme and didn't see his first-born son Jack for over a year after he was born. Then there's the young Alice Quinn who fell in love with and married a young British soldier on the eve of the war. Sadly he was killed at the Battle of the Somme.

Apart from the public events of the time, there are the everyday family stories of survival and joy and wonder. Economically, families tried to be self-sufficient. There's the gamekeeper who shipped batches of freshly caught rabbits to England, children who worked hard on family farms, the small shops and businesses of rural Ireland and the sadness of young people having to emigrate to send home the money to keep large families going. Noel McPartland told me his mother Bridie 'always thought the answer to everything, especially living in Leitrim in those tough days, was to get them off to America. Educate them and send them to

America!' And Delia McDonagh's grandson Frank Gannon told me that Delia emigrated to New York and became 'personal nanny to the Rockefeller kids. She was a nanny and a very good cook, and she was with them for years.'

Weddings were simple affairs, as were honeymoons and setting up a new home. Ninety-year-old Danny Bergin remembers the cost of setting up his own home: 'We furnished our place with a TV and a bed and all and had ten shillings left out of a hundred pound.'

And after the years of conflict, I have followed these families through the generations. Some of them have very specific stories. The Egans of Croghan produced an army Chief-of-Staff, Liam Egan; and a TD, Nicholas. Margaret Tallon has her own memories of helping out in her father's election campaign. There's the story of Tim Crowley who founded the Michael Collins Centre in Clonakilty. Tim told me how the welcome involvement of actor Liam Neeson helped raise funds for a statue of Collins and led to a week-long festival when the pubs ran out of drink and the restaurants ran out of food.

The families I spoke to were all very conscious of the importance of keeping their memories alive and of handing them down to their children and grandchildren. There were carefully saved letters and photographs, birth and death certificates, medals and ribbons, boxes in attics and mementoes of emigration and dances and dreams. In the case of Mary Wallace, born on the family farm in Knocktopher, Kilkenny on 28 January 1901, her nephew had the great idea of recording an interview with her on her eighty-fifth birthday, capturing a voice from the dawn of the twentieth century.

Some of the characters I've written about were well-known figures, such as Frank and Sean Healy, the Egan brothers, Michael Collins and Walter Macken. Here their descendants tell the other side of their fascinating stories, as beloved family members. But most of the people in this book you will never have heard of before, the everyday people of a country coming to grips with nationhood. I hope you enjoy meeting them!

1

The McPartland Family

A WORD TO THE WISE

'My mother always thought the answer
to everything, especially living in Leitrim
in those tough days, was to get them
off to America. Educate them and
send them to America!'

In 1923, Kevin O'Higgins, then the Minister for Home Affairs described the 'Dáil courts', 'Republican courts' or 'Sinn Féin courts', which had been abolished in 1922, as an 'improvised system of justice' that:

> ... *was forged more as a weapon against the British administration in exceptional times and exceptional circumstances than as a definite system which would meet and answer the needs of normal times.*

I am meeting one of County Leitrim's illustrious sons, Noel McPartland, whose grandfather, John McPartland, was a judge in those courts.

'He was a judge from 1918 until the Civil War started. It would have been illegal in terms of the English system. They would be court-marshalling some fella for something and he would be the judge at that particular trial, signing documents and all that. He supported the cause right up to the treaty. He was anti-treaty.'

Later he worked as a haulier, mainly collecting and delivering coal from the Arigna coal mines.

The McPartlands opened their newsagent's and confectionery shop in Drumshanbo in 1885 and kept it going until 1994 with Noel's mum running it until she was 90. It became one of the casualties of the Black and Tans' visit to the town, however, when they burned it out in 1922. 'My father, Hubert, worked in the shop but he was also a hackney driver and the Black and Tans heard

Family shop, Church St, Drumshanbo, 1954, with Bridie, Noel and Aunt Mary.

that he had driven some of the local IRA fellows to a meeting in Ballinamore. The front door, which was also the entrance to our house, was blown in, they destroyed the stock and set fire to the shop. The attack happened at night, the family were all in bed but they got out safely as the fire was confined to the shop. Of course there was no fire brigade at that time, it was the bucket brigade. Buckets of water put the fire out. They also damaged my father's car, which was also his livelihood.'

My father, Hubert, worked in the shop
but he was also a hackney driver and
the Black and Tans heard that he had
driven some of the local IRA fellows to a
meeting in Ballinamore. The front door,
which was also the entrance to our house,
was blown in, they destroyed the stock
and set fire to the shop.

But the Black and Tans didn't stop with the McPartlands' shop, going on to burn several premises in the town. 'They burned a house up the road near the church, a man who was very involved in the IRA. They burned his house to the ground, and almost burned the occupants as well but they were got out on time. They were completely uncontrollable.

People were very much afraid of them. They were the dregs of an army that was sent over here. They went around and abused people, beat people up for no reason, and that was everywhere, not just Drumshanbo.

'My father was on de Valera's side. Dev gave a great speech here in 1932, I have a film of it. It was during the 1932 election. My father was a de Valera man all his life.'

> They were completely uncontrollable.
> People were very much afraid of
> them. They were the dregs of an
> army that was sent over here. They
> went around and abused people,
> beat people up for no reason.

Afterwards, Hubert and another man from the local cumann, Willie Moran, were delegates at the treaty talks in the Mansion House in Dublin. Then Hubert married a local girl, Bridie, who had emigrated to America in 1925. She visited home in 1927 and met Hubert and returned for good in 1930. When they married – in the Pro Cathedral in Dublin – they moved in and ran the shop. They had six children, three girls and then three boys. Moira, 90, is a St Louis nun in California; Frances is 88 and living in

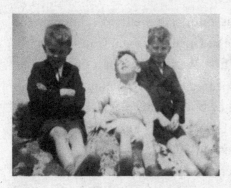

Noel and Sean McPartland, with their neighbour Terry McManus, on the fair green in Drumshanbo.

New York, and the youngest sister, Rosalie, died in 2017. 'Then we have the three boys – Noel and Sean (I'm a twin) and the youngest, Ronnie. Because my mother and a lot of her brothers emigrated in the 1800s and early 1900s, my mother always thought the answer to everything, especially living in Leitrim in those tough days, was to get them off to America. Educate them and send them to America!' And Hubert had the unenviable task of driving most of his children, one after another, to the boat in Cobh, County Cork, or later to Shannon airport as they emigrated to America.

'Moira went first, she went out there on the missions. After Sean, my twin brother, did his Leaving Cert in St Mel's in Longford (that's where we attended boarding school), he went to America in 1956. I stayed on here for another couple of years doing different jobs, and then I emigrated in 1958; I went to Chicago and then on to New York. My younger brother, Ronnie, lives in Howth – he's a retired Aer Lingus pilot. He went to school in the Franciscan college in Gormanstown, County Meath. His class was the first class in it when it opened. The school had been located in Multyfarnham in County Westmeath, but they bought this place and he was in the first class in about 1954. Sean and I are 85, and Ronnie has just turned 80.'

Noel remembers his parents as 'a great couple, very religious, very into their family. We had a good childhood, even during the tough years. My mother didn't suffer fools gladly, now; she didn't like anyone who was trying to pull a fast one. She was a very tough lady. She had to be.'

Noel completed his Leaving Certificate and started his working life in 1951 as a junior assistant master around Drumshanbo. Back then, women had to retire from teaching when they married, so there were plenty of opportunities for a young, newly qualified teacher in the local schools. Noel was living at home with his parents at the time and he remembers one particular night very well. 'We were listening to the radio, it was Radio Luxembourg, and there was a knock on the shop door. It was one of the coal miners from Arigna, in his twenties, but a big man. "Come on," he said to me, and we walked up the street. We got into a car and travelled to the home of another miner in Ballinathera where our job was to collect gelignite that had been taken from the mine. I was sweating! He opened the boot of a car and there were five or six sticks of gelignite in a bag. I immediately asked what would happen if we were stopped on the way home. "Don't worry about it," he said.'

When Noel returned home, the door was locked and he had no key. His father was sitting up waiting for him.

'"Where were you?" he asked me.

'"Up the town," I replied.

'Then he gave me a slap on the side of my face and sent me spinning into the shop. I got caught up with these guys and my father saw and he knew who they were. Then I told him what I had been doing and thank God I told him. He gave me the best advice ever. He said, "If you're caught with those guys again, you may go to jail, but you will never come back here." That woke me up. He had been through it all in the twenties; he had seen it all. He wasn't a man to talk an awful lot about those things.'

Noel had already been introduced to the IRA through his friend's brother but he says their main interest was in having access to a car! He recalls the evening he was introduced to John Joe McGirl in a pub in Ballinamore. 'I remember walking into the pub and the place was packed. My friend's brother introduced the two of us as "two men who wouldn't be afraid to shoulder a gun". We just looked at

one another – our interest was in the car! After the
meeting we went to a marquee dance in Mohill. Later,
we got involved in the 1957 general election and we
canvassed for McGirl, who topped the poll.' Noel says
feelings were very high following the killing of Seán
South and Fergal O'Hanlon on New Year's Day in
Brookeborough. The two were part of an IRA military
column that planned to blow up an RUC barracks in
the town. But it was a botched operation, and in the
ensuing gun battle South and O'Hanlon were shot
dead by the police.

Noel still has his father's ledgers. He was a man of
few words. When Noel and his twin brother were born
in the Rotunda hospital in Dublin in 1936, the ledger
entry is simply 'Dublin with Mother' and on his return
to Drumshanbo three days later, 'Drumshanbo with
Mother'. No mention of
the twins!

Noel says they had a
good childhood but he
and his twin hated school.
'School was really a jail.
Sean and myself were
sent to boarding school
in Longford, and we were

Noel in the army.

noted renegades.' Their parents would send them to boarding school for the three months coming up to Christmas 'to get rid of us; we would go in September until Christmas Eve and then return home'.

Noel's own American odyssey included working in the Hilton hotel in Chicago and being drafted into the US army around the time of the Cuban crisis; he spent five years in the military. 'After boarding school,' he says, 'the American army was like a holiday!' He spent 30 years working for Lairds Jams in Drumshanbo and was named 'Leitrim Person of the Year' in 2019 for his work in supporting the development of the old site into 'The Food Hub' and the establishment of 'The Shed', home of Gunpowder Gin and the first distillery to open in Connacht in over a century.

2

John Vahey

RABBIT SHOOTING AND BLACK AND TAN RAIDS

'They searched up the chimney for
guns, they slashed the mattresses, they
kicked the wardrobes in, they broke the
legs off the table and chairs, everything
that was breakable they broke.'

That was how John Vahey described the raid by the
Black and Tans on their home in Clooncormac,
a cluster of houses between Ballinrobe and
Claremorris in County Mayo. That's where John
and his wife Julia (née Malley) raised their eight
children, including John James, whose daughter
Mary Finlay remembers the fifties, as a child.

'My grandfather was an accomplished gamekeeper and I remember as children we'd be going

to school, and we'd meet him on his way home on his bicycle from shooting rabbits. He'd have the gun strapped over his shoulder using the belt of his coat, and he'd have a little canvas bag to hold the rabbits. He wore a peaked cap and he would always stop when he saw his grandchildren, and he would always have change in his pocket. I can still see myself getting the thrupenny bit with the hare on it.

'I'm not sure where my grandfather started out, but I think it was in Kilrush House, where he trained as a gamekeeper. That's in Mayo. He was reared a couple of miles from there. His wife Julia came from a nearby townland, Ballina. When he married and had children, there was accommodation for a family going in a local big house, so he went to work in Hollymount demesne. The demesne had a gate lodge inside huge big gates, and my granny used to say, "It's right beside the Protestant church and graveyard!" She hated the sight of it. She used to tell me as a child when we would walk past, "Don't even look in the gates there, *a grá*." She often used words in Irish.

'My grandfather used to visit other big houses, either to see what they were doing, or for them to see what he was doing, and it was through that he came in contact with and developed a friendship with Lord Oranmore and Browne. Now Lord Oranmore and Browne was married to a Guinness and he was

John Vahey, gamekeeper.

the father of Garech de Brún of Luggala in County Wicklow. As a child, I remember Lord Oranmore and Browne, who lived in Castle Magarret, coming to our house. He had the shooting rights to our land and that of the neighbours and that went on until the sixties. Grandad was always well turned out. He wore two- and three-piece suits, always a light colour, light-brown tweed, with a butterfly shirt collar.'

John was a hard-working man who got his own land when the land from Clooncormac House was being divided by the Land Commission. They called it 'striped land' in Mayo. 'It was described as about a hundred acres,' Mary says, '30 acres of arable land and 70 acres of horrible land! You couldn't go into it apart from the couple of months in the summer. A small child would be lost in the rushes. During the summer, cattle would graze on it; there were bits of it that weren't too bad. It wasn't really bog.'

Mary's grandfather was a great storyteller and

she remembers long evenings when he always had an extra story for the children. It was an oral tradition; people could read and write to a certain extent, but they didn't have much education. They had quite a smattering of Irish, particularly her grandmother. The stories would go on for hours and Mary's mother Bridie (née Walsh from Clooneareen, Ballinrobe) would say, 'Can I not get you to bring in the turf?' 'And we'd say,' says Mary, "Wait until we hear the next story!" We'd all be round his knee, listening. My grandfather was absolutely lovely, child-centred and kind. I suppose he was Mr Nice Guy! He would sit on one side of the fire, with the crane and the pots and that, and later it would be a solid fuel cooker, and Granny would be on the other side in her chair. And he would be telling us the stories, and if there were any words that she considered to be rude she would say, "You'd be better off saying your prayers!" He was quite deaf, so she'd have to raise her voice. So that was the advantage of living in the house with him. I was about 15 when he passed away.'

Mary's parents had moved in with the grandparents and they had seven children: Julia, Mary, Catherine, Paddy, Sean, Peter and Breege. Mary was born in 1948, 'and my grandfather died in 1964. He was an old man then, 90 years old, but he was a gamekeeper almost to the end. He still had his bicycle and it was he who shot the rogue deer that were causing havoc wrecking fences, vegetables and crops all over the neighbourhood, and that was only weeks before his eightieth birthday! There was venison on the menu for family and friends for weeks!

'Most of our land was game-preserved for Lord Oranmore and Browne, so he wouldn't shoot any game on that; he would shoot predators like foxes, and rabbits because they were food, and pigeons that were eating grain or damaging crops. The staple diet we had was rabbits or pig meat, and fish on Fridays.'

But it was Mary's uncle, Patrick Joseph, who inadvertently brought the family to the attention of the Black and Tans. Patrick Joseph had died young and his death notice was published in the local newspaper. 'He was the only member of the family to be involved in the IRA and because this was referenced in the death notice, maybe they thought the parents were involved as well.'

Author Micheál Lally in his book *The Tan War: Ballyovey, South Mayo*

"We have loved him in life, let us not forget him in death."

Sweet Heart of Jesus, be Thou my love.
—300 days each time.

Jesus, my God, I love Thee above all things.
—50 days each time.

In Loving Memory

OF

PATRICK VAHEY,

Clooncormack, Hollymount,

Who died

26th February, 1922,

Aged 17 Years. R.I.P.

"Sacred Heart of Jesus, have mercy on him."

"May the perpetual light of Thy glory shine on him."

Memoriam of Patrick Vahey.

writes about Patrick Vahey's activities when he was only 16 years old and a runner for the IRA.

The raid on the house in Clooncormac is still a very raw memory. 'The Black and Tans were in the area and my grandfather was working in Clooncormac House,' Mary says. 'My grandmother and some of the children were farming, and my dad [John James], who was only 12 at the time, was minding either just the house or there was a child in it as well. The Black and Tans raided the house, and he didn't want to leave it, but they came in and wrecked everything they could and even searched up the chimney. It was because the house was recognised as an IRA family home; they had evidence of it, it was in the local paper.

'My father was forced to leave the house; he didn't want to, but they forced him out. "Where's your father?"

'"At work."

'"Where is your mother?"

'"In the fields."

'"Go get them."

'And he didn't want to go, which makes me think that maybe there was a baby in the house, but in the end they forced him. So he came out the door of the house, down the front path, but he wasn't moving fast enough, and as he got to the front path, a Black and Tan tipped him on the bottom with his bayonet, and he always had a little scar on his buttock where he cut him. A child. And he's now running, there are no other houses close by, he's going for his dad and his mam, across the main road, he's running as fast as he can, absolutely breathless. He often told me that he was so breathless, that when he met his dad, coming home, he wasn't able to tell him what had happened.

'Word had reached the big house, which was about a mile away, that the Black and Tans were in the area, and his dad, knowing that there was a child, or children, left in the house alone, was on his way to check on them. The other children were in the fields with their mother. They [the Black and Tans] absolutely wrecked the house.

'My grandfather arrived at his house and the raiders were gone and the house was wrecked. He was absolutely furious. He went back up to his boss, Mr Gildea. He had often had discussions with his boss about the Black and Tans and his boss would say, "My countrymen would not be involved in such atrocities", and he would repeat that from time to time. He was an Englishman, but he and his wife were well liked in the area.

'So my grandfather went back up to him and said, "If you want to see what your countrymen are capable of, you can see my house!" And Mr Gildea came down and looked at the house and he was absolutely appalled at what he saw. So he brought my grandfather back up to the big house, harnessed up a horse and cart, and they took furniture from the big house, piled it up in the cart and brought it back down to my grandfather's house. Absolutely decent of them. When I was a child, I always wondered why we had big huge dressers and wardrobes, far too big for the house! We had massive wardrobes that took up two-thirds of a wall, from floor to ceiling, with nooks and crannies and shelves. There were huge big oak chests of drawers and beautiful iron beds, you know the wooden frame with springs tacked onto it? And horsehair mattresses. Other families didn't have that, they had very soft mattresses, but ours were very solid.

'Mr Gildea fitted out the house for us. There was a rocking chair there, I think it came from the big house too. It's probably still around, or maybe it fell apart. We were only allowed to sit in it, supervised, for a gentle rock and then off again. My grandmother did appreciate the furniture and they went on rearing their family. It must have been a very tough time. Mary, the eldest, had left home and married, and Patrick, after a long illness, had passed away. Patrick would have been one of the breadwinners.'

Of the eight children, Michael went off to be an inspector with the fisheries. And my father John James got the farm. Julia died as an infant. Martin was a mechanic, and he joined the Royal Navy. He was in England from an early stage. Peter and Bridget both emigrated to England much later.

Despite his run-in with the Black and Tans, Mary's grandfather never became involved in politics. 'He was always straight as a die. His mantra was that this is what you do, you don't do anyone any harm, you don't speak ill of anyone, and if you can help someone, you do.

'That raid was talked about and talked about. The only thing is, I never saw the scar on my father's butt, but he talked about it at length!'

But there was a lot of unrest while the Black and Tans remained. 'There was a story going around about an area, near the gates of the two big houses, Clooncormac House and Bloomfield House. There was a wooded area where the roots of a tree were, and underneath the ground had given way. It was almost like a little cave and some of the locals were hiding there for days on end, watching and waiting for the Black and Tans so they could ambush them. They heard there were Black and Tans coming on their horses or maybe with a lorry, and they were watching for them there.'

But even when the Black and Tans were gone, the locals had to survive the restrictions of two world wars. During the Second World War, the Vahey family made a living from the farm and 'lamping' rabbits.

'They tied them together by the feet in batches of six, with a label on them, and delivered them to the railway station in Claremorris to go to Dublin. Then they were shipped onwards to England. My dad and his brothers would be out all night, catching the rabbits, panching them – that's where they slit the stomach and take out some of the more offensive parts of the gut so they would travel well. They put a slit on the paw, and they would thread one paw to another so that each rabbit was connected and they would label them. A brown label with a little pink disc to strengthen the hole, tie it on with string, and address it to wherever it was going.

'They could have caught 50 or 60 rabbits by the morning. Somebody would have a motorbike – Martin, he was the guy who was into the motorbikes – and it was six or eight miles to Claremorris, and they'd be on the first train leaving the west. They would sleep during the day and work all night with carbine lamps. They would shine the light on the poor little rabbit, and they would just stay there. This was way before myxomatosis. That didn't happen until the late fifties.'

But the Vaheys ate well, as they were almost self-sufficient. They grew oats for animal feed, potatoes, parsnips, turnips, cabbage, carrots, lettuce, scallions and onions. 'We ate well, and if there was anything that we had plenty of, we shared with the neighbours.

If our cabbage was small and not ready for cutting, our neighbours' might be better and they would share. When I say neighbours, they could have lived half a mile away. There were houses scattered all over the country, next door was at least 500 yards away.'

We ate well, and if there was
anything that we had plenty of,
we shared with the neighbours.

Mary remembers her grandmother as 'a very strong lady. She was the one who had the farming knowledge, because she came from a small farm. Sometimes an uncle coming from London would tell you stories. Uncle Peter would say, "You remind me of your grandmother, she was a strong lady. Did she ever tell you about the day there was a rat in the back garden?"

'And of course, the man with the gun was gone out – there was always a gun in the house. Nobody was coming to protect her children from the rat in the garden, so she took out the gun and shot the rat herself! That must have been some shot, to be able to shoot a small thing like that from the back door. She got teased mercilessly afterwards because one grain of shot went through a tin basin somewhere in the vicinity, and back then you'd have to patch up a tin basin.'

Nobody was coming to protect her
children from the rat in the garden,
so she took out the gun and shot the
rat herself! That must have been some
shot, to be able to shoot a small thing
like that from the back door.

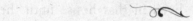

Mary got to know her grandparents very well because they all lived together. But it was hard work for the grandchildren. 'Some of the land had improved; it would have been drained by hand. There was many a day I spent with my back bent over it. There was a drain that went into the river Robe, and this drain was deepened at some stage so that it would flow better. It was up to us to dig our own little drains in our land so that the water would flow off. So you dug a little drain – the adults would do most of it, but the children would help, little children lifting stones was invaluable in man hours! We would dig a trench, probably 8 to 10 inches deep, and we would put two rows of stones down each side of it, leaving a gap in the middle, and then you got the longer stones and formed a little bridge.'

It kept the children occupied and, as Mary points

out, there was no television to distract them. 'And we knew why we were doing it, so there would be no big pond the next winter and the grass would grow. Then in the 1970s my brother, who had been in Australia on a two-year passage, came home with lots of money and he bought a JCB, and he put these yellow pipes with holes in them into the land and drained a lot of it. So now, probably 90 to 95 per cent of it is good land and being farmed.'

John James Vahey lived in that house until the day he died in 1999 at the age of 89. His son Patrick still lives on the farm.

Throughout the fifties, the children all walked the two and a half miles to school and, as John and Julia Vahey had had eight children, there were lots of cousins as well. 'I went to school in Roundfort,' Mary says. 'To get to Roundfort, I had to walk through the nearest village which was Hollymount. It didn't have a church, and it didn't have a school – quite a few pubs though! And a shop or two and a pump for water. We walked right through there, past the graveyard, across the railway line, and a couple of hundred yards past that was the school and the church.'

It was a tough journey for a small child but, as Mary says, 'We didn't know any better! My parents selected that school because the whole road to it was a tarmacked road. If we had gone in the other direction, to Newbrook school, we would have had to use a sand/gravel road. We had shoes or boots and we brought lunch, and something to drink. Usually milk, in a bottle. A small Guinness bottle, maybe. And we'd have a sandwich made with homemade brown bread and whatever was going in the house at the time, whether it was jam, cheese, egg and rarely meat.'

For people who lived so close to the land and so close to nature, death was never a taboo subject. John Vahey told a story from his youth, 'about a guy who died sitting up in a chair and nobody found him until the next day, so when they went to lay him out, rigor mortis had set in and they couldn't straighten him! So they put him onto the bed, strapped his legs onto the bed so the legs wouldn't lift up, and the same thing on each arm, so he looked quite straight in the bed. And everybody in the neighbourhood gathered to give him a send-off. The women

John and Julie Vahey with two of their children, Patrick and Mary, c.1906.

said decades of the rosary, and there was a barrel of porter. They took out the plug and poured it into jugs. And on that particular night, the ladies were all around the bed saying the rosary, and one of the guys who knew that the corpse had to be kept straight was at the side of the bed and he released the rope, and the corpse slowly lifted up! And that was a great story. It would have been a great scandal that nobody had been checking in on the old man and he had been left dead in the chair.'

The ladies were all around the bed saying the rosary, and one of the guys who knew that the corpse had to be kept straight was at the side of the bed and he released the rope, and the corpse slowly lifted up!

And people were prepared for death. John's wife, Julia, kept all the necessary requisites for a funeral in the bottom drawer of an outsized chest of drawers. Mary remembers 'brilliantly white sheets, kept white by washing regularly, once a year, in the springtime, when there was frost. And they would be laid out on the grass because the frost would keep them white. Laid out flat on the grass overnight, so that the next day, any kind of yellowing that had occurred over the months would be gone. Tablecloths would be put out too, because tea stains would be removed or seriously diminished in that way too. And then there would be a white quilt, a woven quilt with fringed edges, and a pillowcase with fringing too. And that would be for the bed that the corpse would be laid out on.

'My granny in her older age – she wasn't feeling well, she probably had a bit of dementia and she would be rambling a bit – she thought that we were her brothers and sisters. She was 84 when she died, but from about 80 on, she wouldn't be quite sure. My mother, Bridie, was so good to her and they got on so well. My grandmother would say, "I want to see my father and mother", and my mother would say, "OK, I'll bring you", and she'd open the door and bring her out, down the path, out the front gate, ten yards along the road, in the back gate, in the side gate and back in the front door. And she'd say, "Now, there we are, that was a grand little walk", and Granny would sit down and be happy.

'Mam was very kind like that, a great way with people. And because she had lived in England, right through the war, she had a lot of life experience that other people didn't have. She worked from when she was 18 to 28, in Manchester. When she went there first, she went as a servant in a house. The lady of the house would show her what needed to be done,

how to answer the telephone, how to set the table
properly, things you wouldn't learn in a thatched
house with no napkins and limited knives and forks!
She got a job in a hotel then. She worked in a hotel
right through the war, and moved her bed down
into the basement, because it saved getting up in the
middle of the night when the air-raid sirens went
off! You got ready in your room, went downstairs in
your dressing gown and slept in the basement.'

Bridie met her husband, John Vahey Junior, when
she came home to Ireland to visit her family and they
persuaded her to stay because the bombing was so
bad in Manchester. She stayed at home for almost
a year and met her future husband at a dance in
Ballinrobe. But it wasn't love at first sight because
she dated his brother, Michael, for a while!

After about a year, she went back to England and
she stayed there for at least another year or two,
to make money, while the war was still on. They
corresponded by letter. 'As a child,' her daughter
Mary recalls, 'I would have seen the letters that
would have been opened by whoever opened letters
back then, and anything that mentioned the weather
would have been crossed out in black pen, because
apparently you weren't supposed to mention it for
security reasons! We begged her not to burn the
letters, but she said no, they were very personal, and
she destroyed them all.

I would have seen the letters that would have been opened by whoever opened letters back then, and anything that mentioned the weather would have been crossed out in black pen, because apparently you weren't supposed to mention it for security reasons!

'The wedding was all arranged and then the groom-to-be became ill and spent some time in hospital and the wedding was postponed. They eventually got married in November 1945. Bridie came home with a trunk full of clothes, her wedding trousseau. It was very hard to get clothes at the time as you needed coupons to buy them. But her friends had rallied round and shared their coupons. There were long-time residential guests in the hotel she worked in and all of them had given her wedding presents! I still have a Czechoslovakian glass bowl that was given to her as a wedding present. The other things I remember were a silver container with blue inserts with four little dishes in it, tiny spoons as well as some Carlton ware. All of that was brought to Mayo in a trunk.

'At her wedding, Bridie wore a teal blue dress and coat with a little hat. She had some lovely clothes and she always had a handbag that she carried with the confidence of a woman who had been out in the world and lived in the middle of a war, although she rarely spoke of her experiences during that time in Manchester.

'They got married in Ballinrobe church early in the morning and came back to her father and mother's house for the breakfast. Then she moved into the house with her father- and mother-in-law. That was a big thing to do for a woman who had had her freedom for so long. As a child you don't appreciate that. I remember when my grandfather died in 1964, she was a different woman. It was now her house.

'And it was a busy house, there were seven children and four adults. My younger sister was four when Granny died, I was 13. And I was 15 when Grandad died. She died a few years before him, and his heart was broken. He cried for days. There was a concrete seat where the sun shone in the mornings, and he would go down and sit there and my mother would

John Vahey Jnr, with his new bride, Bridie, and his parents, John and Julia.

say, "Oh God, look at him sitting there on that cold seat", and she would go down and persuade him to stand up so she could put a cushion under his butt. He was tall and very pale; he would sit there and cry and cry, the tears would be running down his face, and nobody could console him. He missed her dreadfully. They must have been married for 60 years; it's a long time. They had eight children and buried two of them. And that would have been unusual at that time, to only lose two babies.'

Mary never met her maternal grandmother, Kate Gunnell, who on the death of her first husband married Mary's grandfather, James Walsh. Kate had three children from her first marriage to Mr Hyland and then seven. 'My mother was the eldest [of the eleven]: Bridie, Michael, Tom, Jimmy, Willie, twins Nora and Margaret, and Kathleen. Her children [from her first marriage] Jack and Mary Kate Hyland lived long and industrious lives while their sister died at a young age. Her nightdress caught fire, she had very bad burns, and she died a few days later. And sadly little Margaret, who was a twin, died from diphtheria during an outbreak of the disease in the late 1920s.

'They lived in Cloonearneen in Ballinrobe in a little thatched house, two bedrooms and an open-plan kitchen cum living area. Kate was very competent on the sewing machine. She made her living by collecting a bolt of tweed and a bolt of calico from the local shop, and she made men's suits and shirts. She was a tailoress. That was what she was capable of doing and that is how she was able to rear her children. Payment was very little, it may have been pence or a shilling per suit, but she was allowed to keep whatever fabric was left over. Presumably she got good at cutting out!

'At some stage, not very long after her first husband died, she married her sister's brother-in-law. Two brothers, married to two sisters, living in Cloonearneen – they called it a village but actually what it was was a cluster of about twelve houses, mostly thatched.

'They had a small parcel of land and James [Mary's grandfather] worked the land and cut turf. He also had potatoes and a beautiful orchard with a lot of apples. I'm not sure if he just sold the produce or if he made poitín himself! This was back in the twenties. If someone snitched on you because you were doing something illegal, there would be a payment. Somebody in this little village was watching what he was doing. One day of the week, he would harness up two donkeys and two carts, and put the potatoes and the turf and the poitín and the apples on, and he would go the three miles to town to sell his wares, either going around the street, or he had somewhere that he would stop and people would

come to him, or he called to particular houses to his
weekly customers.

One day of the week, he would harness
up two donkeys and two carts, and put
the potatoes and the turf and the poitín
and the apples on, and he would go the
three miles to town to sell his wares.

'He gathered that maybe he was being snitched
on, so what he would do is harness up the donkeys
– he would be in charge of the one in front, and
he would tie the reins of the second one onto the
back of the front cart, and he would walk the mile
and a half to the tarred road, which was the main
Ballinrobe to Claremorris road. He lived well off
the beaten track in a little sand road with the grass
going up the middle. Then he would swap the
donkeys and put the white donkey in the front cart
and the dark donkey in the back cart. So when he
was searched in Ballinrobe, and quite often he was
searched, they would only search the cart where the
white donkey was – which is what the man had
snitched on, presumably. He was never caught.

'If they had a bit of bog and a worm it would have
been easy enough to make the poitín. If there was
smoke going up it could have just been that they

James and Kate Walsh,
Bridie's parents.

were making tea or whatever. So that was how they lived their lives in a little thatched house! That house is no longer there. My uncle and aunt gave it up in the seventies, when they were given a house and land by the Land Commission in Naas, County Kildare, and the land and the homestead was divided to increase the holdings of the other people in the village.'

3

The Two Mollys

IN LOVE WITH MICHAEL COLLINS

*'They were all in love with
Michael Collins, all of them!'*

Molly, Margaret, Mena and Trina. This is the story
of four generations of women, starting in the
1920s with Molly Spratt, a 'runner' for Michael Collins,
told to me by her granddaughter Mena O'Connor and
her great-granddaughter Trina O'Connor.

In 1920s Dublin there were two Mollys, Molly
Spratt and Molly Darcy. They were well-known
street traders and also secret runners and carriers
for Michael Collins and his men who were fighting
both the regular British army and the Black and
Tans. They ran messages; they would hang around
near the Metropole cinema or the Rotunda hospital
area and the men would appear from tunnels and
drop something in their lap as they walked by.
They would cover it or put it in their smock and

deliver it to Collins, in one of his secret places. One of these places was a house on Brendan Road in Ballsbridge. They walked from Summerhill over and back, together or separately. They were part of the underground movement of women during the War of Independence. They also used their skirts to hide supplies, often sewing bullets into the hems of coats and the long skirts that they wore.

Molly Darcy and Molly Spratt were often mistaken for cousins, but they were not related.

Molly Darcy was the grandmother of Bill Cullen, businessman and author of *It's a Long Way from Penny Apples*.

These two women were trusted members of the movement, who would help get food, letters and ammunition to the rebels. Because they were street traders and door-to-door sellers, they could easily move between the north and south of the city without suspicion. They had to work together on this and couldn't let anyone know what they were doing for fear of being informed on. It was said that they could talk and talk without taking a breath. They worked as runners from 1916 onwards.

One day in 1920, the two Mollys were walking down O'Connell Street. Molly Spratt had her three-year-old daughter Margaret in the pram. The Black and Tans were on patrol and running amok. They stopped the two women and questioned them, and then lashed out with the butt of their guns to hit them, but they missed them and hit the baby in the pram.

I'm meeting Mena O'Connor, the daughter of that baby in the pram, and she tells me that her mother carried the scar of that day all her life. 'The pram was often used to carry weapons to the rebels. They used to have the kids in the pram and have stuff underneath them, weapons, notes in milk bottles, in little parcels in the milk itself. The Black and Tans stopped the two women and questioned my grandmother, Molly. She must have answered them back or something because they lashed out at her, but they missed her and hit my mother in the pram. In later years, when she was asked about the scar, mother would say, "The Black and Tans done that." Well, she wasn't quite that polite when she answered! I don't know if they would have known any secrets, because it was very undercover and covert and all that, but that was their job, to keep these guys going, and keep the information going between them. And they were all in love with Michael Collins, all of them!

> The pram was often used to carry
> weapons to the rebels. They used to
> have the kids in the pram and have stuff
> underneath them, weapons, notes in milk
> bottles, in little parcels in the milk itself.

'The two Mollys had another friend, Kathleen Hart, who was also very well known. On one occasion, they got a message from a family that was being evicted, so the two Mollys and Kathleen turned up to meet the men about to carry out the eviction. Molly Spratt was armed with a heavy pot, Molly Darcy with a heavy pan, and little Kathleen Hart had a rolling pin. They flayed at the men and even hit some of them. The men did not retaliate as they knew who they were and who they were connected to and they were feisty women. The women told the evictors not to come back, and they went off and left the family in peace!'

The two Mollys were known as the two strong women, and if they saw somebody struggling, they would do their best to help them, Mena told me. 'There was a story about the Black and Tans coming into the 27 Steps in Summerhill and attacking a gang of children. I used to dance up and down them as a child, counting them. My mother would have done the same thing. The Black and Tans used to run down those steps and lash out at everyone – they were just wild. My mother would have to leap out of the away, hiding in the areas underneath the houses. They called that the "Area", under the tenements.

'Molly Darcy was known as "The Mother" because she had seven children and was widowed at 36. Alongside Molly Spratt, she took in children and orphans until she could get someone in the area to take care of them. They were known as women on a mission, and they would do anything to make a few bob ("makes"). They would go to Howth to get fish and sell it or buy fruit and sell it off the prams. But they were very generous and shared what they had with other women – if someone needed a shilling for gas or a bill they would send it up to them.'

Molly Spratt (née Donoghue) was born on 22 May 1895 in the Rotunda hospital. She lived in Gormley Buildings off Sean McDermott Street and in 1913 she married John O'Reilly and he joined the Royal Fusiliers in the same year. John was killed on 20 October 1914 in Ploegsteert, Belgium. He was posthumously awarded a victory medal and a star and clasp medal. Molly was pregnant with twins when the news of John's death reached her, and on hearing the news, she miscarried the babies.

Molly's second husband was James Little from Monaghan and he was a Protestant. He was known as Larry and was a tic-tac man at the races. 'My mother remembered going with him to the races

Molly Spratt.

and trying to salvage some of the money from him
to bring back to my granny. Larry was a dapper
man and always dressed up. Their first home was
in Buckingham Street and later they moved to St
Joseph's Mansions. They had six children and Molly
always worked.

'My granny would make sticks and sell them
around the big houses on the southside of the city.
I remember as a child cutting up old tubes from
bicycles and making rubber bands for the sticks and
going around the houses selling them. She also kept
pigs and chickens in a shed in buildings opposite the
now Fitzgibbon Street garda station – there are flats
built there now. She would rear the pigs for Christmas
and sell them to the butchers in Moore Street.

My granny would make sticks and
sell them around the big houses on
the southside of the city. I remember
as a child cutting up old tubes from
bicycles and making rubber bands
for the sticks and going around
the houses selling them.

She would leave a bucket in the mansions for
people to put their "slops" into and she would send
me to the big houses for the slops.'

Molly was also the go-to woman when the ladies went into labour. 'To this day I still meet people who tell me that my granny delivered them. She had a set of white sheets, that was her tools. She told me stories of the custom of giving babies to couples within families and neighbours if the mother was too sick to take care of the newborn. Sometimes these children were returned to the birth family, but sometimes they stayed and were reared there. She also personally took babies in until the mother was well enough to look after them. I also recall her telling me about bringing the dead babies to the Angels plot in Glasnevin.

> She told me stories of the custom of
> giving babies to couples within families
> and neighbours if the mother was
> too sick to take care of the newborn.
> Sometimes these children were returned
> to the birth family, but sometimes they
> stayed and were reared there.

'She was also the woman who would lay out the bodies for the wake and subsequently got a job with Jennings funeral home in Amiens Street. I was living in Donnycarney around 1959 with my family and when there was a death in the locality, I would be sent running to the local phone box to call granny. She would duly arrive with her kit, candles, crucifix and holy water. Many a time she brought me with her to lay out the bodies. I was very young, about eight, certainly too young to be seeing dead bodies. She'd say, "Grab that sheet, put that there, get the cotton wool." I was like her little protégé or apprentice; she knew I wasn't squeamish. We'd have to have coppers for their eyes, to keep the eyes down and all. It wasn't scary, it was just part of it.'

When Mena was a child, her grandmother Molly lived at number 28, Summerhill. 'They were the tenements, I recall them as being big huge rooms with very high ceilings and an open fire, and a load of children in the same bed. There was a scullery off the main room and I remember the Carnation milk, tinned milk. Molly loved a glass of Guinness or a large bottle of stout. Across from where they lived, there was a pub called the Rose Bowl or something like that, and they used to get some relief going there after their day's trading. Later she got a flat at 29a St Joseph's Mansions, a new-build at the time. They left the tenements behind but the tenement life was a very free life for children. We all played round there together.'

But Molly had her own problems. According to Mena, several times 'she called the guards on her second husband when he assaulted her. He arrived

Madge Joyce, the Molly,
Molly's granddaughter Rosie and son-in-law Johnny.

in court, all dressed up as usual and commented to the judge, "Look, this is what I have to put up with", referring to Molly challenging his behaviour. He was imprisoned in Mountjoy in 1921. He was buried in Glasnevin. My grandmother left strict instructions not to bury her with him. She is buried in Balgriffin cemetery.

'My father was Johnny Joyce. He was born in the lane where the Cadbury's site is now, in Coolock. That lane was called Doherty's lane, and his father lived in a cottage on that lane. The cottage is still there now, beside the garda station in Coolock. They sold the land off to Cadbury's for five pounds an acre at the time. My father was afraid of nobody. He was one of twelve children, whose mother died on the birth of the twelfth child. He was put into a home, and he had scars of the cat-o'-nine-tails on his back from the home. The home was down the country somewhere. In order to get the children out of the home, my grandfather had to marry this woman who was about to become a nun. Her name was Mary. He had to have a mother for these children, to get the children back.

> He was put into a home, and he had
> scars of the cat-o'-nine-tails on his back
> from the home. The home was down the
> country somewhere. In order to get the
> children out of the home, my grandfather
> had to marry this woman who was about
> to become a nun. Her name was Mary.
> He had to have a mother for these
> children, to get the children back.

'He was a very angry man, but he was a very good father. Well, to me anyway, because I was the champion Irish dancer. My grandfather was afraid of my father. So when Molly was getting hidings and beatings, she would run to our house in Donnycarney, and my father would go in and sort it out.

'My mother Margaret, or Madge, was very posh; she was from the north-east inner city and she was super intelligent, she had such a bright mind, and yet she had no access to education.

'Yet she used to do the crosswords in *The Irish*

Times, they used to run competitions for it, and she used to do it upside down just to make it a bit harder. She used to win competitions in the *Independent* for crosswords – she won loads of grandfather clocks!

'We're really a family of street traders. I retired from Fairyhouse Market in the last ten years. I was there for 25 years; I graduated from selling second-hand stuff to buying and selling cosmetics. My first memory of selling was in my mother's tea rooms, near the Ferryman pub. The banana boat used to come in there, and I was three or four so we're talking about 1955 or 1956. My father was a builder's labourer, so he was gone off to work, and my mother used to have to bring the children to the tea rooms because there was no one to mind them. The older ones were all gone off to England at this stage. I would be brought in, and the sailors would come in with the bananas. And we would take the bananas and give them tea and boxes of matches or whatever they needed. I couldn't reach the counter, so my mother used to have to stand me on a little wooden box that the TK minerals came in. And I'd be standing up on that, fascinated with these sailors coming in.'

And even as a child Mena was inventive when she needed money to go to the cinema on a Sunday. 'I'd go round the houses and collect the milk bottles, the neighbours would keep them for me, and if I got a tray of milk bottles, I'd get 4 pence for the tray.

The pub up the road had soda siphons, and I would collect them ... and golf balls! Clontarf golf links was beside where I lived, and I climbed a great big wall and scoured that golf links with my brothers. We would clean up the golf balls and sell them around the doors. Our summers were spent picking fruit in Donabate and bringing the money home to Mam.

> I'd go round the houses and collect the milk bottles, the neighbours would keep them for me, and if I got a tray of milk bottles, I'd get 4 pence for the tray.

'So from that, I would go down to Moore Street with Molly with the fruit to sell it. At Christmas time we'd be outside Arnotts on Henry Street, as they do now, selling our Cheeky Charlies and all that. My children would be there too, selling "10 for a pound, the wrapping paper!" I loved it. *Loved* it. It's in my DNA to sell, I'd sell anything.'

Mena's uncle Seamus, who was Molly's son, married a woman called Maura from the North. 'She came from the North carrying a little bundle with her. The only place that they could find to live was the tenements in North Great George's Street. But they lived in the hallway because they couldn't get a room and you'd have to pass by them to get in. There was just a tap on the stairs they used for water. There was one toilet out the back they used for everybody. I remember dancing up and down those stairs, playing and singing a song about the snowy mountains. And even then they were kicking people out of the hallways, that was in the late fifties. They went to London then for a few years. Maura was well thought of in the family and was actually my godmother.

'When they returned Seamus was in a pub in the city and he had a bundle of notes, showing off, and there was a man beside him, a Scots fella, and he followed him home. At the time, he was living in a laneway off Temple Street hospital. And this man followed him home and slit his throat for the bundle of money … and it was no money, it was a fiver wrapped around a bundle of newspaper! The Scotsman got the mandatory life sentence of 25 years, which was later overturned and he was released.'

Mena's daughter Trina believes the women in her family were 'women on a mission. They saw social injustice and wanted to be part of the movement against the British oppression of Irish people. From what I can recall talking to my Nanny Joyce [her paternal grandmother] she was very much a republican. We brought her to see the movie *Michael Collins* and she was shouting at the screen in the cinema, "Gwan Michael! Gwan Michael!"

'When you ask about their motivation, I think survival, but from their hearts, when you look at the

Molly Spratt.

type of things they did, they protected other women. They saw the oppression of women in this Catholic Ireland, and the oppression of people in Ireland from the British occupation. They were very much on the side of the oppressed because *they* were oppressed. And their conditions ... they were so poor but also they were very socially minded. My grandmother and her sister Nelly, they grew up very community-motivated too, they set up ladies' clubs. My mother was very involved in community development; I'm involved in community development. It's in us all, to help the downtrodden. I think the motivation for Molly, my great-grandmother, was that she was downtrodden too. She met a lovely man who by all accounts she loved, and he was killed in the war and she lost her twins. She then married her second husband, who treated her terribly. So the only thing she could do was get involved with more powerful men as a form of protection, the Michael Collins connection. She aligned herself with powerful men, as a protection.'

She met a lovely man who by all
accounts she loved, and he was killed in
the war and she lost her twins. She then
married her second husband, who treated
her terribly. So the only thing she could
do was get involved with more powerful
men as a form of protection, the Michael
Collins connection. She aligned herself
with powerful men, as a protection.'

Trina says one of the things still talked about in the
inner city is that the women who acted as runners in
the twenties were never recognised for what they did.

Mena did a secretarial course and worked in
Brooks Thomas. Then, as all good stories begin … 'I
fell in love and moved to London. I was pregnant and
I wasn't married so I couldn't stay here. I worked in
an accounts department in London. I had my baby,
got her minded, and they asked me to go back, and
I went back when she was six weeks old. I was there
till I left London, in 1973.

'My partner Charlie O'Connor joined the British
army and he deserted after six weeks! He deserted
because I was pregnant with our second child, Trina,
and he wanted to be with me. Then we decided to
come back to Dublin. We were all bundled up in this
second-hand car, the cot and pram and everything,

and we got to Holyhead and Charlie was arrested for deserting the army. And we weren't married! And I couldn't drive, so I was coming back to Catholic Ireland, with a baby, pregnant with another, and Charlie was incarcerated in prison in Wales.

'They had to push the car onto the boat. I was on the boat vomiting, and this woman takes the baby off me – she could have run off with the child, but she wouldn't have got far on a boat! She minded the child for me while I was sick. So when we got into Dublin port, my father-in-law, Flats O'Connor, another fascinating man, he picked me up with his friend who could drive, and we got the car home, and I lived in their family home just up the road from where I live now, with 14 children. They had 14 children and a few babies. But the positive side of Charlie spending six months in prison was that he learned his trade as a bricklayer.'

In the meantime, Mena had moved out of the house with the 14 children and squatted in a flat in Ballymun. 'I was lying on the floor, no bed, nothing. My sister lived in the next block of flats and her husband kicked the door in so I could gain entry. I had one child, Adele, and I was pregnant with Trina and I had no furniture, not even a clock. I had a little camp stove to make scrambled egg every day. The only way I would know the time in the morning was I'd see the dockers going to work. I wasn't married so I couldn't get any benefits. We had savings from London, but I couldn't get access to the savings – they were in a joint account and Charlie was in prison!

I was lying on the floor, no bed, nothing. My sister lived in the next block of flats and her husband kicked the door in so I could gain entry. I had one child, Adele, and I was pregnant with Trina and I had no furniture, not even a clock. I had a little camp stove to make scrambled egg every day. The only way I would know the time in the morning was I'd see the dockers going to work. I wasn't married so I couldn't get any benefits.

'He came home in November, and that day he went down to the priest in Ballymun and organised for us to get married. On the Saturday morning I was getting married, the 24th of November 1973, I went to my sister in the next block, and I said to her, "I need you to come to the church with me." St Pappin's in Ballymun, it's closed down.

'And she said, "What do you need me to go to the church for?"

'"I need you to be witnesses. I'm getting married."

'And she says, "I thought you *were* married!"

'The church was locked the day I got married –

they wouldn't let anyone in just in case they saw me, because I was seven months pregnant. I was married at the side altar.

'We squatted in a few places, in Ballymun and Kilbarrack, but I badly wanted a house for my children. I was told the only way I'd get a house was if I evicted myself from the house we were squatting in. So we had to put ourselves out into the front garden into a tent, and the council put a family into the house while we were in the garden with the two children! The next-door neighbours used to take the girls at night and we would stay in the tent. And finally we got a house in Darndale and later succeeded in getting a transfer to this house in Artane. I've been so happy here, it was what I wanted, there were beautiful old neighbours who fussed over me.'

> I was told the only way I'd get a house was if I evicted myself from the house we were squatting in. So we had to put ourselves out into the front garden into a tent, and the council put a family into the house while we were in the garden with the two children!

4

The Kavanagh Family

A PASSION FOR
THE REPUBLIC

'The family was offered compensation,
one pound for every year of her life.'

Mary Ellen Kavanagh was 19 years old when she got caught up in a bank raid in the town of Buncrana on 4 May 1922. A bunch of irregulars raided the bank, the shooting started, and when Mary Ellen went out to lift up a child in the street she was hit by a stray bullet. She took a fortnight to die in Derry hospital. One half of her family believed it was the bank raiders, the irregulars, who fired the shot that killed her, whereas others say it was the pro-treaty people who were coming up the street. 'It could have been either side,' says Peter Kavanagh, Mary Ellen's nephew, the renowned journalist and former editor of the *Dundalk Democrat* and brother of legendary photographer, the late Paul Kavanagh.

Mary Ellen was one of a family of 15 children, eleven of whom were girls. Her sister Sarah stayed with her in the hospital and was with her when she died. There was no inquest into the shooting; the only inquests being held at the time were into military affairs. The family was offered compensation, one pound for every year of her life, so they received 19 pounds. There is a monument to her memory in Buncrana opposite the scene of the shooting and in 2015 a plaque was unveiled at the site.

Mary Ellen's older brother, Edward, 22, was greatly affected by her death and it propelled him into taking an active part in the Civil War. Edward was given a commission as captain of the 'A' Company of the 35th battalion of the National Army. He got his commission from Richard Mulcahy, whom he never met. 'The main character in Dundalk in that period was Frank Aiken, who later became Minister for Foreign Affairs; they called themselves "generals". He was in the first division of the IRA, and he took over Dundalk military barracks in April 1921 from the last British garrison to leave Dundalk. The British garrison had played a huge role in life in Dundalk for nearly 200 years and leaving Dundalk was a big step.'

Peter Kavanagh is Edward's son, and reminiscing with him is like sitting around a table with the fascinating characters from his family long ago, a family that had its roots in Donegal, Derry and Dundalk.

Constable Horner and his wife, Mary.

'I don't know a lot about my father's side as a child. His mother's people were called Lynch, and they came from a rural part outside Buncrana town. One of the first things he told me was that he was sitting on a hill, watching the grand fleet steaming into the Swilly, in October 1914.

'My mother Rosaleen (née Horner) had a different background entirely. Her father had been an RIC man, then he left the RIC and became an insurance man in Derry. His son Jim had gone off to join the RAF when he got word that the War of Independence was going on and came back to Derry and got terribly involved. He was particularly perturbed about the arrival of the Black and Tans in 1920. Jim returned to Ireland and got a job in Northern Ireland's civil service in the Ministry of

Labour. He became a passionate republican, which led to his arrest in May 1922 after he was observed wearing an IRA uniform and removing a Union Jack from the house of a Protestant family. The Horner home was raided by the "B Specials" but this may have been down to his sister Rosaleen, who was a motorbike dispatch rider for her local Cumann na mBan battalion. Jim was arrested and taken to Derry jail and on June 22nd he was interned on the prison ship the *Argenta*, which was anchored in Larne harbour. Jim spent 15 months on the ship and insisted on being treated as a political prisoner. He was released in December 1923 and moved south of the border. But between leaving the ship in September and their actual release, some of the prisoners, including Jim, were held in Derry jail. Some of them were beaten up, and this led to a hunger strike. Jim's health deteriorated and he was given the last rites and the news was passed to his family that he had actually died.

He became a passionate republican,
which led to his arrest in May 1922 after
he was observed wearing an IRA uniform
and removing a Union Jack from the
house of a Protestant family.

'My mother, Rosaleen, was Jim's older sister, and she had visited him when he was on hunger strike, and she also visited other IRA prisoners in jail at the time. Jim survived it all, but he died in the 1940s from the treatment meted out to him while incarcerated.

'Afterwards, Jim lived in Dublin and got a job in the civil service when the de Valera regime came into power. He would remain very pro-republican and died as the Second World War was ending. Rosaleen always remained very fond of him. They had two other sisters, Nora and Dolly, both of whom had been working in Dublin for the British regime. In 1922, they were given a choice. They

The Kavanagh family – Nora, Chrissie, Dolly, their mother Mary, Jim and Rosaleen.

could work for the Irish government or they could get a job with the British government. The eldest, Nora, went to London and worked with the British Department of Defence. Dolly stayed in Dublin and worked in the Statistics Office.'

Peter says his family connection with Dundalk began in 1928 when his father Edward arrived in the town with his wife. 'They had been married in 1924 in Derry Cathedral. He had joined the gardaí after leaving the National Army. The Dundalk he arrived in was in a state of turmoil. I was born on McSweeney Street, which was only just built. It was a new development by the council then. Dad had a peculiar career in the early twenties. He had been involved with the IRA from about 1918 onwards. How he got involved I'm not entirely sure, but he told me he was an "oath-bound" member of the Irish Republican Brotherhood in Donegal.

His chief mentor was a guy called Joseph Sweeney, who fought in the GPO in 1916. He always abided by what he had to say. Dad claimed, rightly or wrongly, that he himself was the commander of training on Inishowen peninsula and he had been forced into hiding in the mountains. He arrived back in Buncrana, his home town, in 1921 and that is where his involvement with the National Army began.

'The extraordinary part of the story is that my

Edward and Rosaleen
Kavanagh.

mother had been active in Cumann na mBan in Derry
city, and she had sided with the anti-treaty side. She
had been in Drumboe Castle when one of Dad's
units attacked the castle on behalf of Joe Sweeney.
She must have known him before that period.
My mother was actually two years older than my
father and had learned Irish at Cloghaneely College
in County Donegal and may have met Pádraig
Pearse. Her Irish was so good that my grandmother
described her as a native speaker!

'I'm not sure if that was correct! But that was
the Blayney influence. Neal Blayney stayed with
them as a lodger and I think he might have primed
my mother and her brother to get involved with
the revolution.' Neal Blayney went on to become
a commander of the IRA in Donegal during both

the War of Independence and the Civil war. His son, Neil, was born in Donegal in 1922 and had a distinguished career as a Fianna Fáil TD and served as Minister for Posts and Telegraphs, Local Government and Agriculture and Fisheries.

Interestingly, Peter says there are many stories about the disruption caused on the railways in Donegal by armed women. 'There was one famous incident where a woman got on the train and threw all the English papers out the window!'

Peter's father, Edward, had grown up on the family farm where his father, John Kavanagh, had a contract to supply produce to Drumree fort, to the British. 'That's how he got a knowledge of the running of the British garrison at Drumree fort. I don't think my grandfather was too happy that his son was consorting with the rebels. John's wife, Annie Lynch, was a shopkeeper.'

Peter says the first time his dad told him anything of his activities was when he spoke of the 1918 December election. 'He recalled that he was playing snooker in a hall in Buncrana when the word came through that Sinn Féin had won so many seats, and the hills on both sides of the Swilly were ablaze with bonfires as their supporters celebrated. This was the first indication he gave me that he had been involved.

He recalled that he was playing snooker
in a hall in Buncrana when the word
came through that Sinn Féin had won so
many seats, and the hills on both sides
of the Swilly were ablaze with bonfires as
their supporters celebrated.

'Then he told me about the burning of the
courthouses in July 1920. A week later, a bunch of
Black and Tans arrived, camped outside Buncrana,
and raided all the houses. There were arrests, but
Dad got away! Dad loved to tell the story of how
he had petrol and spread it and set fire to the
courthouse, and then the doors slammed shut, and
they thought they were all going to be burned to
death. But they managed to escape and get away
anyway.

'The man who was in charge in Buncrana was
called McLoughlin. Dad always regarded him as a
sort of a hero. After the burning of the courthouse,
they headed off into the hills and somehow Dad got
to Glasgow, where he spent about 18 months. He
seems to have been supported by the Glasgow Celtic
club. Later, he had a job in Derry city as some kind of
taster of teas with a tea importer. I don't know how
he secured that position. When he was looking for

a job Dad had been asked what he had done before he joined the army, and he put down "On the run".

'My mother always told the story that her first-born, in 1925, had died at birth as a result of not getting to the hospital in time. Then in 1929, twins arrived; they were born in a Dublin hospital but my parents were actually living in Dundalk. Then I was born, then my youngest sister in 1940. So that was our family.

'Dad had been what was known as Special Branch, set up in Dundalk by the Cumann na nGaedheal government at the time as a sort of armed force. Dad never joined the old comrades and he never joined the Blueshirts, because he didn't agree with O'Duffy in Monaghan. He hadn't a good word to say about de Valera until the fiftieth anniversary of 1916 when he got a letter from him. I thought it was one that everybody got, but he read the letter and he said to me, "Maybe I misjudged the man." I never saw the letter, but when he died, in his papers were details of an incident when he had been delegated to guard de Valera when he was in Dundalk, and they were worried that people who didn't agree with Dev would be out to assassinate him. The date was sometime before 1935. There was also a typewritten document – this extremist group in Dundalk wrote their own constitution! They were called Saor Éire.

'I'm pretty sure Dad never met Collins, but Collins had the status of an almost saintly figure.

Our window was broken by supporters of Fianna Fáil when they won the election in 1933 – they hurled stones through it. My mother was never critical of them and my dad just took it as part of the times they lived in. There was a lady named Mrs O'Hagan who he was very fond of, who would have been on the other side – but it emerged that she had saved his life. Assassins had been sent from Belfast to kill him, sometime in the 1930s, and she'd gone to the train station and told them, "You can't shoot Ned Kavanagh." That was the sort of crossover that was going on at the time.'

Our window was broken by supporters
of Fianna Fáil when they won the election
in 1933 – they hurled stones through it.
My mother was never critical of them
and my dad just took it as part of
the times they lived in.

And when it came to Peter's own childhood he says he was 'educated by rebel clergy, rebel in that they weren't very parochial, they had their own thoughts. They were split into the ones that supported Parnell and the ones who would have

Pauline and Paul Kavanagh.

been against Parnell. I must say now, when I went to work, the man who was my boss said, "Never join an organisation that asks you to take an oath." That was strange, but it was great advice, because I was approached to join the Knights of Columbanus. Dad showed me a little card he had, a membership card, and he said, "When I joined the guards, we were instructed that we had to resign from those organisations. To my great regret, I discovered that all the guys who got promotion had not left the Knights."

'Another strange story that emerged after my father's death was that sometime in the 1940s Dad was missing from the barracks. They rang headquarters in Dublin wanting to know where he was but were told, "You'll do nothing about that, he's on a special mission." And it turned out that he had gone to Derry docks and taken his son Paul with him, a child, and taken the names of the American warships that were in the harbour to send to the Irish government. So he acted as sort of a spy, which I never knew about.'

Peter went to school in St Mary's College, Dundalk. 'But what I didn't realise was that it was a kind of a seminary. During the day, religion was discussed freely in the classrooms. There were 33 in my class doing the Leaving and 12 of them went on to be ordained as priests. Most of them stayed the course; I think only two of them left. Religion played a huge part in our education. When we left school, a friend of mine, just one friend, went to university. He studied commerce, I think. When he came back, in 1956, we joined a debating society in Dundalk. I remember it well. One fellow came up from Rathmines School of Journalism and told us the basics of how to deal with public speaking. The interesting point was that women came to the meetings and said nothing, until one day one of them stood up and spoke and then they all wanted to speak, and they ended up running the whole thing. And they were far better at public speaking than the men!'

> During the day, religion was discussed
> freely in the classrooms. There were 33
> in my class doing the Leaving and 12 of
> them went on to be ordained as priests.

Paul Kavanagh was 12 years older than Peter and went on to become an esteemed photographer, although he started out as a journalist with the *Democrat*. When Paul left the *Democrat* to work with the *Irish Independent*, Peter got his job and remained with the paper for 50 years, retiring as editor. 'I retired at 66, I wanted out. I covered everything. I didn't realise anything was special until it was over. The time that Ben Dunne was kidnapped, I was sitting in the office and I got a call from a garda source and he said, "There's a great story from the border. A customs fella saw a car being stopped just across the border, and a man being dragged out of it." For some reason or other, they knew it was Ben Dunne. I sent the story to BBC and RTÉ, and the next thing I got this call from one of the editors in RTÉ, and he asked me where I got the story. I said I couldn't tell him, and he told me that he knew it was correct but that there was an embargo on it and that I shouldn't have released it. So I said, "That doesn't affect me!" The story ran and ran for weeks. I never met Ben Dunne but I got a few bob out of it!

'I was going to tell you about another story – there wasn't much money in it, though. A lot of the media came to Dundalk but they wouldn't go over the border, and they'd ask you to go out and have a look. The locals would know me and I would get away with it to some extent. But myself and another chap, Kevin Mulligan, went out to Carrickarnon and there were lorries burnt out at the side of the road. This would have been in the 1970s, and Kevin said, "What are these brown candles doing here?"

"Be careful, Kevin," I told him, because I had seen guys with these things earlier. "I think that's gelignite." Later in the day I went up to Newry and there was a big hole in the ground where police troops had come up and shot at it and blown it all up! That was the sort of thing that went on on a regular basis. There was an Irish customs post close by on the main Belfast to Dublin Road.'

Today Peter is still active, writing a column in the *Democrat* called 'Trip through Time'. 'I didn't intend it to be that way, but after I retired, the editor, Joe Carroll, asked me would I continue writing pieces. I was in the habit of writing local notes, which were a mixture of local history, local happenings and all sorts of things. Newspapers are nearly finished now though, I think.'

Peter married Margaret Kellehan in the early 1970s and they had two children, John and Sarah.

Peter is also very close to his nephew, former RTÉ journalist Conor Kavanagh. 'When Conor was small he used to come with me in the car. That's how he got involved with reporting because I used to be going places and visiting incidents. In August 1971 he famously filmed the Battle of Courtbane for me. During the incident a British soldier was shot dead in an ambush of a British army convoy. It happened between Louth and south Armagh. I had to go back into town for some reason and so Conor stayed and filmed it. I think that's where he got his love of journalism!'

Conor Kavanagh remembers it well. 'I went with my father, Paul, who was a photographer and shot 16mm film for RTÉ. Two British army Ferret scout cars, light armoured vehicles with Browning machine guns, crossed the border and went a mile into the Republic, in an apparent map-reading error. When they reversed and tried to return across the border a large crowd of local people in their Sunday best surrounded the vehicles and prevented one of the armoured cars from driving away. One of the scout cars was attacked and an attempt made to burn it.

'I witnessed an IRA unit, men in berets and green army parka jackets, loading rifles into the boot of a car and running across fields to take up firing positions on a hillside. There was heavy gunfire, some returned by the British army, who were observing the scene in a helicopter, and one British soldier was shot dead. Gardaí and Irish army personnel were at the scene and took cover but did not or would not intervene. The gardaí seized the damaged vehicle and it was towed in to Dundalk. It was later returned to the British authorities, who claimed the fatal shots were fired from the Republic's side of the border and that Irish troops were slow to respond to the attack by the four-man IRA unit.

'I lay behind a sand lorry to take cover while the gun battle raged. My father hid behind a heavy concrete gatepost at the side of the road and captured some iconic photographs of gardaí running up a country road to escape the gunfire and close views of local people clambering over the damaged Ferret scout cars. I was a schoolboy at the time and was not at all concerned, though the tragic loss of a young soldier's life did not seem right, as he was just a little older than me. I had thought the British army had been sent to Northern Ireland to protect Catholics from loyalist pogroms.'

5

Eileen Scanlon

A HIDDEN MESSAGE

'If she had been caught,
she would have been shot.'

In 1919 against the background of the War of Independence, 20-year-old Eileen Scanlon lived on a small farm outside Dungarvan in County Waterford with her parents, Richard and Alice, and her ten siblings, six girls and four boys. At that time girls didn't go to work outside the home unless they went into service in a big house, *if* there was even a big house in the area. So the women did all the work in the house and looked after the men. Eileen's daughter, Colette Cox, is telling me about Eileen's life as a messenger for the republicans.

1919 was a year of turmoil. In January, two Royal Irish Constabulary officers had been shot dead while escorting a load of gelignite to a quarry in County Tipperary, Dáil Éireann had had its inaugural meeting in the Mansion House in Dublin even though most of the members were in UK prisons, and in February Éamon de Valera made his escape from Lincoln prison with the assistance of Michael Collins.

Eileen was a young recruit to republicanism and, Colette tells me, seemed to be singled out all the time for carrying messages. 'But if she had been caught, she would have been shot. This is how it worked: somebody would write the smallest amount of information on a piece of paper, as small as a stamp, and her mother would do her long hair for her, up in a bun, and she would hide the piece of paper in the bun. She was very uneasy, Granny was always very uneasy, because all it would have taken would be for one of the Black and Tans to ruffle her bun, and she would have been caught and shot on the spot.

This is how it worked: somebody
would write the smallest amount
of information on a piece of paper,
as small as a stamp, and her mother
would do her long hair for her, up in
a bun, and she would hide the piece
of paper in the bun.

'They devised a system then. When her father and her four brothers were out working on the farm – it was a small farm, it just kept them fed – Eileen would get two bottles and fill them with tea. One bottle had just plain tea and milk in it, and the other had milk and tea and sugar, and she would make sandwiches. She would make one special sandwich into which would go the tiny message written on brown paper. She would cut the crusts off that particular sandwich so that when she was handing them out, she could identify the one with the message in the middle.

She would make one special sandwich into which would go the tiny message written on brown paper. She would cut the crusts off that particular sandwich so that when she was handing them out, she could identify the one with the message in the middle.

'Eileen used to take her two bottles of tea and bag of sandwiches and walk out into the field where the brothers and her father and the neighbours were working away. She deliberately did that so she would have their protection. Whoever got the sandwich without the crusts on it, they knew they had a job to do. She would maybe put a person's initials on it, like "CC6", and that would mean they were meeting in that house at 6 p.m.

'She was never caught; well, she was intercepted a few times, but she was only carrying bottles of tea and sandwiches out to the fellas in the field. Somebody might have passed these messages on to her mother or father, and she would pass it on to somebody else, and it would do the whole circle before 6 p.m. They would all have to get to whatever house or barn that they had to meet in. It was a scary time.'

All the men would be out working
the land and the women would be
in the house looking after the meals
and the men, cooking and washing
and ironing and all that. Polishing the
fellas' shoes for Sunday mass! That was
their place; they wouldn't have been
annoyed about that. That was life.

Eileen had six sisters: May, Peig, Hannah, Bridie, Kitty and Lil. 'That's the seven girls. And then there were Jack, Paddy, Richie and Toddy.' Colette describes the family farm as 'very basic, they had no machinery so everything would have had to be done with the spade and fork. All the men would be out working the land and the women would be in the house looking after the meals and the men, cooking and washing and ironing and all that. Polishing the fellas' shoes for Sunday mass! That was their place; they wouldn't have been annoyed about that. That was life.

'The family had one cow that kept them in milk. They farmed potatoes and carrots and turnips, things they would have eaten themselves; they wouldn't have had much more than that, but they were lucky to have it. Things were reasonably comfortable. The women made all the clothes, though, clothes for the men and for themselves. There wouldn't have been sewing machines, they would have been made by hand. They had hens and chickens, and maybe two cows because there were so many of them. They made their own butter.

'I was wondering how did they cook cabbage. They would have cooked it in the pot with the meat, but how did they strain it? Or did they just scoop out handfuls of cabbage? There were no strainers back then. They might have just put it in the potato pot and let it dry out. I always had visions of the heap of potatoes for twelve people sitting in the middle of the table, no such thing as a bowl. And they wouldn't have been peeled, they would have had to peel their own potatoes, so that would have been another pile on the table. I don't think they ate the skins – Granny never ate the skins. But nothing was wasted, the skins would go into the bucket for the pig feed.

Eileen Scanlon.

'None of the houses had showers or baths or running water. They didn't wash, they just smelled! You can imagine a house with 13 of them, with five of them men out in the fields all day, working. I would imagine they would have worn boots out in the fields, whereas the women would have been in their bare feet working at home. It would have been a hard life, 13 of them and no electricity.

'All of the brothers would have been in the IRA but not the women. But you've got to remember that they were down in Waterford, so things would happen six months before they would even hear of it. They had no radio or telly, nothing. If somebody didn't write and tell them, then it never happened!

But you've got to remember that they were down in Waterford, so things would happen six months before they would even hear of it. They had no radio or telly, nothing. If somebody didn't write and tell them, then it never happened!

'Regarding the meetings they held in one another's homes, it would have been something like they were planning on ambushing the British army, maybe trying to knock a few of them off their pedestals. It was pretty violent at times: there were incidents where British soldiers could be killed but then that would result in the British soldiers shooting about ten of them. They would be random shootings, not like "Oh I think that fella is up to something" – it would be "Oh there's a few of them, let's shoot them."

'All of the girls would have delivered messages in turn, not only my mother, and the lads would have tried to make life difficult for the British army, burning down stations and that kind of thing. I wouldn't say any of them would have killed any of the soldiers, though. I don't think they really got their hands dirty. It was just more making life difficult for the British army, without getting caught or being held responsible. That's why it was so secretive, because they would have been shot if they were caught. That's why Eileen liked being able to carry the messages – it gave her something to do against the people she hated. She was so angry about the British being here. Always, always. Even when she was older.

'The brothers saw no future for themselves on the small farm, no possibility of supporting a family of their own, so they all decided to leave. One of them went to America, Paddy, and the other three lads went to England. Grandad Richard was too old to do much on the farm without the help of the four lads. So he sold up the farm and he and Alice moved to England to be with their children. They moved from one house to another and apparently Alice was the greatest troublemaker, because she'd bring stories from one house to another and cause trouble. Richard eventually got Alzheimer's, but nobody knew what it was back then, and he kept getting lost on them! They were sort of cross with him, God help him, but sure he didn't know who he was.

It used to really annoy Eileen that
although she had been born in
Ireland there was a crown on her
birth certificate which meant,
technically, that she was British,
and that didn't go down well at all!
I think she felt that she had
been downgraded in her own
country by foreigners.

'They were all over the place in England. Kitty and Lil were in Surrey. Eileen, my mother, kept in contact with Kitty and they lived together. They were great friends. But neither of them settled and so they only stayed for a few months. It used to really annoy Eileen that although she had been born in Ireland there was a crown on her birth certificate which meant, technically, that she was British, and that didn't go down well at all! I think she felt that she had been downgraded in her own country by foreigners. And then, of course, the Custom House went on fire in 1921 and so she had no birth certificate anyway as the records all perished in the fire. We used to tease her about her citizenship, it was terrible. We'd say, "You're English – there's a crown on your birth cert!"

'Auntie May, who was the eldest, she was like Mrs Bucket. Kitty and her husband Paddy, from Kerry, would come over often, with their three kids. They met in England but went back to live in Ireland. They used to come over on the ferry, the five of them. Paddy had been incarcerated on a prison ship in the twenties. He was from Kerry, but when he came to Ireland he would only come as far as Dublin, he never went near Kerry. I think he didn't want too many people to know he was here. He was involved in the IRA; it wasn't the crowd that are there now; they were a bit more idealistic back then.'

All the Scanlon girls got married. 'Poor Lil met a fella at a dance and she married him six weeks later. She knew very little about him and later discovered that he had been a Christian Brother. Auntie May was the eldest sister. She married a fella from Cork. They all married Irish people who were as poor as they were!

'They didn't have homes of their own in England but Paddy Lyons, who eventually married Kitty, had a house and I think they all sort of camped in his house until they got places of their own. They spread around after that, wherever they could find work. You have to remember that there were no phones back then so you'd have to write letters to keep in touch. Poor Granny Alice, there was no way she was going writing eleven letters. She'd write to May, Lil and Kitty. They sort of stuck together, not out of necessity, but because everyone enjoyed May's carry-on. For example, she didn't have a hallway like the rest of them, she had a "lobby". You may wonder why they all went to England and not Dublin but there were no jobs to be had there. But in England they were building and constructing and there was plenty of hard work to be had.

'Eileen eventually met and married my father, Michael Magner, and they had four children: Anne, Susan, myself and Aileen. Michael came from Kilrush in County Clare and he had two brothers, Patrick and Jack, and three sisters, Mary, Delia and Hannah, the youngest. My father was born in 1901 and he and Patrick joined the IRA. One day in 1921 somebody went into their carpentry workshop in Kilrush and tipped them off that they were going to be picked up that night and arrested. They said nothing at work because they didn't know who they would be talking to but they got up on their bikes and cycled home and they explained to their mother that they had to disappear. They packed whatever they had, probably what they were standing up in. They got on the bus from Kilrush into Limerick Junction, and they got the train from Limerick Junction to Dublin, and they stayed overnight in some hotel. That was a novelty to them, because they never would have been inside a hotel before!

'The next day they went up to the depot and enlisted in the Civic Guard, the two of them. They were of good repute, and reached the standards they were looking for at the time. They were tall, they could talk, and read and write and add up. Perfect! The brothers did their training, and Michael was sent to Dundalk, County Louth and Pat was sent to Cashel in Tipperary. They were about 20 and 25 at that time. Michael was in the Depot, so he had more opportunities than Patrick had in Cashel. He was singled out for making models of the various crime scenes that they were investigating, so if there was a murder in a house or a shop or anywhere, he got the job of making the model to scale for the court. There were no photographs or anything back then so the courts would rely on the models he made. He would go to the scene of the murder and measure everything, and come back to his workshop in the Depot. When the court case was over he could do what he liked with the models. So we were always kept well supplied with dolls' houses!

'There was a funny side to it too. Wherever the body had been found, he would draw a red circle on the spot. I remember Anne, my eldest sister, asking my mother what all the red circles were in the dolls' houses. My mother said that they were rugs! She had to answer but she couldn't tell her the truth. I remember Anne saying, before she found out what they really were, "It's very dangerous to leave a rug at the end of the stairs, isn't it?" We had a good laugh about it when it was explained.

'Patrick never moved from Cashel, and probably would have stayed in Kilrush all his life if he hadn't joined the guards. People didn't move away from their own place; it was costly. If you moved to Dublin you had to find a job and get accommodation. But when they joined the guards, they had immediate accommodation in the Depot. Michael's mother died when she was 52, which was very young. He would have stayed safely in the Depot, in the guards. He wouldn't have felt safe visiting Kilrush at that stage, they wouldn't run the risk. That would have been understood by the guards. Sure a lot of them, even the people admitting them into the guards, could have been in the IRA themselves.

'I remember everything in my parents' house was either brown or dark green, it was all painted. There was a dresser that my father made in the room between the hall and the kitchen, and he painted that dark green, and I remember Anne saying to him, "Why don't you paint that a lighter colour and it would make the room bigger?"

'And he said to her, "Then you would see the dirt!"

'And Anne said, "But sure if the dirt is there, it's there! Just because you can't see it doesn't mean it's not there."

'But it turned out he was colour-blind anyway! I remember asking him years later, if he was colour-blind, how did he manage the traffic lights. And he said, "I don't see the colour, I just see which of the three lights is winking." There were no driving tests or driving lessons back then!

'Religion was a huge thing in Ireland in those days. In Kilrush the important people were the priest, the teacher and the solicitor and they were held in high esteem by the ordinary people. The women and the men were kept separate, so when you went to mass on a Sunday, the women went to the right-hand side of the church and the men went to the left. The women had to cover their heads because you disgraced your head if you went into the church without anything covering it. So they probably had no shoes or underwear, but they all had head scarves!

'I remember too, a long time later, I was in school in St Louis in Rathmines in Dublin and we were doing home economics, that sort of embraced needlework, and we had a poor creature who was only a few years older than us but to us she was an old woman. She was teaching us hand-sewing. When Granny and the girls were doing sewing there was no such thing as a machine, it was all hand-sewing. We were all making knickers and I remember someone asking the teacher, "Why are we learning to make knickers?"

And she said, "Well, if there is another war, you'll be able to make yourself a pair!"'

Informal fostering was a popular practice in the early 1900s and Richard and Alice Scanlon had fostered their daughter Eileen with two maiden aunts who lived outside Dungarvan. The aunts were accomplished dressmakers and had their own business. Colette says her mother hated it because it meant she was separated from her own siblings. 'She did gain, because they taught her to be a very good dressmaker – she never would have got that at home. But when she began to realise that she had ten brothers and sisters and she didn't live with them, she would be very sad. She'd go home to her parents in the summer for a fortnight or three weeks, and she loved that she had the other ten kids to play with. When it was time to go back to the two aunts, she would be very unhappy. She resented that to her dying day. She was a baby when they handed her over, and I would say she was with the aunts until she left school, probably at twelve. It was an awful custom.

She was a baby when they handed her
over, and I would say she was with the
aunts until she left school, probably at
twelve. It was an awful custom.

Michael Magner died in February 1982 but his wife
Eileen lived to be almost 100 and spent her last few
years staying with various family members. Colette
recalls a visit she made with her mother, her husband
and two of her children, Miriam and Kieran, to see
Eileen's childhood home in Dungarvan. 'It was a lovely
house, a lovely design, a big huge room with an open
fire and the crane and pot and all. That took up one
whole wall. There was no running water or anything
like that. There was a stairs that went up from the
middle of the floor, and a landing either side of that.'

Colette continued the family's republican tradition
when she met and married David Cox in September
1962. David died in October 2005. But he was one
of the six children of John J. Cox who came from
Derrygonelly near Enniskillen in County Fermanagh
and joined the IRA when he was 18 years old. Four
years later he was arrested for his involvement in
a series of attacks on a number of barracks in the
North. He was imprisoned, firstly in Crumlin Road
jail in Belfast and then on the prison ship the *Argenta*,
in 1921. He was deported from Northern Ireland

when he was released in September 1923. It was a conditional release which meant he was deported to the South and forbidden from entering the six counties for the next two years. And even then he would require permission to go into the North.

John Cox was an only child, and his parents – farmers – disinherited him as they disapproved of his republican activities. He was arrested in his family home at 23 years of age and this was the last time he saw his parents. When he came south he joined the then fledgling gardaí (as had Colette's father) and was appointed to Belmullet in County Mayo where he met his wife, Annie Sweeney. Annie's brother, Ted, was the lighthouse keeper in Blacksod, the lighthouse that changed the course of the Second World War. It was the Sweeneys' weather report that convinced the allies to delay the D-Day invasion for 24 hours. John Cox's last post was as garda sergeant in the barracks in Howth, County Dublin. But there was no further contact with his parents, and his own children knew nothing about their grandparents.

The extraordinary thing is that David's father never mentioned his IRA history or his imprisonment to his family, and it was only many years after John Cox died in 1967 that the story emerged.

Colette and David have five children – Miriam, Kieran, Fintan, Clare and Niall – and seven grandchildren.

6

Máirín Hughes

AN EYE WITNESS
ACCOUNT FROM 1922

'I remember being at the station in
Killarney, waiting for the train, and Daddy
and Mammy got off with the coffin. My
first brush with death, I suppose.'

Máirín Hughes was in her class in the Mercy
convent in Killarney, County Kerry in 1922
when there was an attack on the RIC barracks just
down the road. She was eight years old and remembers
that the class were all kept in over lunchtime. It was
about a mile away from the barracks. 'We weren't
allowed out to play that day and the two or three
children who lived nearby weren't even allowed
home for their lunch. The nuns gave us milk and
sandwiches and then, all of a sudden, we could hear

shooting. The Killarney barracks was being taken over by the Irish. We weren't allowed home until about five o'clock that evening.'

'We weren't allowed out to play that day and the two or three children who lived nearby weren't even allowed home for their lunch. The nuns gave us milk and sandwiches and then, all of a sudden, we could hear shooting. The Killarney barracks was being taken over by the Irish. We weren't allowed home until about five o'clock that evening.'

Máirín had joined the school in second class. 'My classmates were so indignant because I hadn't been put into a babies' class! That was Mammy's idea; she had home schooled me until I was eight. I liked school, I never had a problem with it. When I moved on to secondary school I liked history, I loved poetry too. We didn't do science at all at school. That's why there was a terrible discussion when I said I wanted to do science when I left school. We had a head girl in the school, and we had a Christmas play. I was her daughter in the play, and I thought the world of her. She went to college and she did science and that's why I decided I wanted to do science too. Not a very academic way of looking at it but I took to it like a duck to water!

'Where we lived in Killarney there was a bridge over the Deenagh river just outside our gate. There was a military guard on the bridge during the Civil War because they were blowing up the bridges. I think the guard on the bridge slept in our farmyard, in one of the outhouses.' As a child, Máirín remembers the military activity around the area where she lived. 'I remember an incident that happened about a mile or two behind our house. There was a lorry going along with three or four British soldiers sitting on benches either side, with their rifles. There was a field with people picking potatoes and the soldiers shot at them. One of the potato-pickers fell to the ground; he was shot, but he survived! This would have been about two miles back towards Killarney, sometime during the War of Independence. They weren't popular! But despite the reports, I don't ever remember being frightened by them.

There was a lorry going along with three or four British soldiers sitting on benches either side, with their rifles. There was a field with people picking potatoes and the soldiers shot at them. One of the potato-pickers fell to the ground.

'I remember the Black and Tans alright. I would see them passing. We rented half a big Victorian house, with a big sloping lawn up off the road. You could look down onto the road, onto the tops of the lorries passing by.' She also remembers the esteem in which Michael Collins was held in Cork. 'He was regarded as the chief and held in great respect. We had a picture of him in our house, and everywhere you would go there would be a picture of him hung up in the house.'

Máirín was born just two months before the start of the First World War, on 20 May 1914, 'close to the feast day of St Rita of Cascia, the patron saint of impossible cases'. But it was also nine days before the ship the *Empress of Ireland* sank in the Gulf of St Lawrence with the loss of over a thousand lives. The World Fair was held in Lyon in France in May and the House of Commons was about to pass the Irish Home Rule Bill just fivedays later.

Máirín's father was William Sheehan from Newmarket in County Cork and her mother was Annie Dineen from Rathmore near Killarney. 'My grandparents had a farm, Dad always loved the open air. They had an excellent schoolteacher in that area. In those days the students left school very early but the teacher continued to teach them. He would have them all back in the evening times, after the day's work, and he would teach them the names of the stars and he would show them the countryside or tell them about history. He was a wonderful teacher. Those that were bright enough, he would put forward for different jobs and suggest different things – that's why he suggested my father go into the civil service.

> He would have them all back in
> the evening times, after the day's
> work, and he would teach them
> the names of the stars and he
> would show them the countryside
> or tell them about history. He
> was a wonderful teacher.

'My father was a pensions officer in Killarney. Back then, he had to deliver the old age pensions by hand so that he could check that the recipients were who they said they were. There was no such thing as going to the post office in those days. He travelled all around by motorbike. Petrol wasn't rationed but you were lucky if you could get it. Anyone who had a motorbike or a car was a suspect. Only the doctor or the priest were safe to have cars. Dad had a permit with his picture on it to deliver the pension books to those who needed their money. He did it once a month, but by the time he delivered to the whole area, it was time to start all over again. I have one little memory: Dad was heading off to work one morning and he hugged Mammy and she was crying when he left, because the government offices were being raided and closed down. He was threatened and told to give up his job but he wouldn't because he didn't want to leave the old people without their money. But nothing happened to him, nothing at all. He shared his office with another man, and the other man had run away to hide, but nothing happened in the end; they didn't come near the office. My mother was a down-to-earth woman, an excellent cook and a good housekeeper too.

'I was actually born in Belfast, in Ballyhackamore, a townland in County Down. In school I always insisted I was born in County Down, and they used to say, "Belfast is in County Antrim!" But I was born in the southern district which happened to be in Down. I don't remember anything about Belfast or Dublin, where we also lived for a while. I was two and a half when we moved to Killarney, which was my home until I got married in 1950. My dad came from an Irish-speaking family so he was actually called Liam. I had no sisters and three brothers. Rory was the eldest, then Con, and there were seven years between Con and me, and there were eight years between me and the youngest boy, Sean.'

But the family was beset by tragedy as two of the boys died very young. Rory, the eldest, died when he was 17 from an acute appendix. 'We were living in Killarney, he was taken to Cork, and it had perforated by the time he got there. There were no antibiotics then, so

Máirín Hughes, 107 years young.

he died in about six days. I remember being at the station in Killarney, waiting for the train, and Daddy and Mammy got off with the coffin. My first brush with death, I suppose. That was 1921.'

Then Con died, also of acute appendicitis. 'It was Christmas Day when he got the pain in his stomach, five or six months after Rory. It was during the War of Independence, and of course they couldn't take him up to Cork as the roads were blocked. The military barracks in Killarney got in touch with the military barracks in Cork, and one of them went to the surgeon and told him about it, and the surgeon set off on the Macroom road. But he was turned back, wasn't allowed through. So he tried the Mallow road. Dad being the civil servant, he could go anywhere on the motorbike, so he set off and he met the car and he stopped it. The poor surgeon thought he would be forced to turn back, but it was Dad and he was able to bring him through to the house.

'The kitchen table was scrubbed and carried up to the bedroom, and Con was operated on in the bedroom. The two doctors in Killarney were with him for the operation, one was acting as the anaesthetist. When they opened him the appendix had perforated, so he had peritonitis, and there were no antibiotics back then so nothing could be done. He died about four or five days later. I remember there was a nurse in the house. I was being kept down in the kitchen out of the way. Con was only 16. Rory had died before the Civil War, before the restrictions, so he was taken by car to the hospital in Cork. I remember Con's funeral well. Rory had been buried in the new cemetery in Killarney. And then Con was going in and it was a double grave. When Con was going down, Mammy had her arms around me, and I remember her saying, "I'd love to have a quick look at Rory." I was only eight. My poor mother, it must have been very hard. But I think it must have been harder for my father. Mammy had the young baby, Sean, to look after, she was occupied. The two lads had been old enough to go climbing with my father, they were companions for him, so there must have been a big gap in Daddy's life. Sean was only a few months old then, he was a baby.'

The kitchen table was scrubbed and carried up to the bedroom, and Con was operated on in the bedroom.

Máirín remembers the wakes of her childhood. 'The neighbours all came in, and at regular intervals they would gather round the corpse. The corpse was never left alone, there was always somebody in the room, day and night. The men stayed up during the night. I remember when my father died, in Cork, the uncles were up, and the women were all sent off to bed around eight or nine o'clock. I remember I woke up and I heard my uncle Jack going to the kitchen and making tea and bringing it back up to the men – they all had a good feed in the middle of the night! If there was a sudden or unexpected death, the news was always spread after mass. The people would gather round and ask, "Did you hear so and so died?" And the next question would be, "Did he have the priest?" So in other words, was it a sudden death or was the priest called. That was important, in fact more so than the doctor!'

'The neighbours all came in, and at
regular intervals they would gather
round the corpse. The corpse was never
left alone, there was always somebody
in the room, day and night. The
men stayed up during the night.

Máirín has few memories of the Second World War, which didn't affect her immediate family, but she does have a memory of the shortages imposed by the war and the coupon rationing system. 'There would have been shortages. Clothes rationing, you had coupons and all that. They drove my mother crazy! I remember one day in Cork she saw a lovely piece of material and thought, "Oh yes, that would make a lovely skirt", and she asked for a yard and a half of that, and they said, "That will be three coupons" – but sure she had no coupons with her! She had to leave the material behind. She couldn't cope with that at all, she never remembered to bring her coupons!'

Máirín's own hobby was birdwatching. 'I had a first cousin, she was a doctor down in Kilkenny, she was a birdwatcher and a nature person, and I often went with her on her trips. One year she said, "There's a group in England that are going to the continent, to see the flowers in Austria, and I'll go if you come with me as a companion." So that started my birdwatching life. I went with that crowd several times.'

After she left the Mercy Sisters in Killarney, Máirín went to UCC, from where she graduated with a degree in chemistry. But it was a very difficult time for the family. 'My father developed leukaemia, which was fatal in those days, towards the end of my first year in college, and I must pay tribute to him. I could have been taken out and put into a shop or something, but no. He had started his career as a British civil servant in London, so he had a British civil service pension. But that didn't pass to the widow in those days, so after my father's death (and he was only in his late fifties) my mother had no pension, no income. And even when he was diagnosed with leukemia, he was immediately retired. He didn't get an Irish pension, but there was some friend in the civil service who sorted it out for my mother; she said afterwards that he had done a marvellous job! I remember there was great rejoicing when she did get her pension.

'But, as they say, the Lord opens windows. In the medical school in UCC they needed a chemist for a specific job and I was offered it. I was told I might have to handle blood, and would that be alright? I was getting five pounds for three weeks' work. It was a fortune and it also meant that I was able to help out financially at home while the row about my father's pension was going on. So I went, and I stayed from then until I got married in 1950. After the three weeks were up, I went home to my mother, and she said, "Is that it?" And I said, "I think so, but nobody said not to come back!" So we agreed I'd just turn up on Monday and see how things were, and everyone on Monday said, "Hi, Máirín, how's it going, good to see you", and it was like they just wanted me there, so I stayed. There were very few women in college then, and very few in science. There were two others in the class with me, but I was the only one who went on and did a master's in chemistry.'

Máirín's youngest brother, Sean, went on to college and he did chemistry as well. 'He did engineering first actually, but there were no jobs for engineers at the time (this was during the Second World War years) so he decided that he would go back to college and do something else for the year so as not to be idling. And Alfie O'Rahilly, he was the president of UCC at the time, said, "Sean, don't be stupid. This war will go on for some time. Why don't you do another degree, not just odd bits and bobs?" So Sean did the master's in chemistry! Sean had two children. Nuala is living in England, she's a science graduate as well. She lives in Yorkshire and she's married. And Michael is living down in

Carlow. He is an excellent cook, keeps his house and he's totally independent.'

I asked Máirín how she met her husband, Frank. 'Well, Daddy was very fond of mountain-climbing. He loved going to Glengarriff for the holidays. We had a Ford car to travel in and he just loved the Reeks. Mammy didn't go climbing herself, but she would hire a rowing boat and take us out around the bay and all that. One year there were three young fellas in the hotel in Glengarriff, and we used to go out in the boats and walk around together and all that. Then we went down the next year and there were two of the three fellas there, so it went on from that! Frank was in CIÉ in Heuston station – he was from Sligo – and we got married in 1950. We lived in Palmerstown, so I've been here in this area a long time. I was here before Maryfield [the nursing home where Máirín now lives] was built! I'll tell you a story about that, actually: just after it opened, two little boys were running up the road and one said, "What's that place?" And the other one answered, "That's where them auld ones live!"'

But back to the wedding. 'It was very simple and nice. The ceremony was in St Patrick's parish church in Cork. I wore a navy suit that was bought in Dowdens, which would have been the Switzers of Cork! A navy suit and a white blouse, which was a Donegal special, it was lovely. My mother did all the choosing! And a navy hat with a brim turned back with white satin. The wedding was early – I think the mass was at ten o'clock. Mammy made the wedding cake and we had the breakfast in our own home. It was a quiet wedding, no fuss, not many people. We went to Gougane Barra for our honeymoon, which was beautiful. It's at the source of the River Lee, and that's where St Finbarr lived, he was the patron saint of Cork. It's quite a small lake with mountains on three sides. A place of pilgrimage for Cork people. After the honeymoon we moved to Dublin and set up home in Palmerstown.'

One of the great sorrows of Máirín's life was losing her two babies in miscarriages. 'I carried them, but I lost them. I never saw them. It was very sad when no more came after them. A lot of babies died then, I suppose. There was a fair lot of adoption too, but when I talked the idea over with Frank, I gathered he wasn't keen on adoption. I felt a reticence there. "Alright," he said, "do it if you want to." But I thought both of us should be a hundred per cent for it or it probably wouldn't work. So we didn't go ahead.

'It wasn't the done thing for married women to go back to work in 1950, but during the flu pandemic of 1957 a friend of mine came to see me. She had been in college with me, she did arts, she was teaching in the vocational school in Crumlin.

She was a widow, and she had two sons. She said, "Máirín, we are absolutely stuck for a teacher. Would you ever come in and do just two or three days?" Frank knew her, and when she left he asked me what she wanted. So I told him that she asked me to go into teaching, and did he ever hear anything like it. And he said, "Do you know what, you should help them out and go in for two or three days while they're searching for someone else." Sure I went in and I stayed teaching until I had to retire! About 17 years, I think. The extraordinary thing was that I was only in, and Frank died within twelve months, and there I was fixed up with a permanent job and a salary. God opened marvellous gates for me! I taught in Crumlin for a short while and then I moved to Ballyfermot, and that's where I retired from.'

Máirín has always had an interest in religion and is a secular Franciscan and a member of an apostolic group which meets regularly. One of their tasks was sewing vestments for priests travelling on the missions. 'We don't make vestments now, but there was a time where we would make vestments, fill a case with everything a priest wanted going on the missions. Altar cloths, small linens, finger towels, a complete set of vestments, the whole lot. I have so much to be thankful for, and I appreciate it very much. Like Susanna in the Bible, we are living in the house of the Lord.'

Máirín wears a 'tau', a letter in the Greek language. 'In the time of St Francis, it reminded him of the Cross, and he accepted this tau as the Franciscan emblem.'

Máirín is UCC's oldest living science graduate and in November 2018 she was honoured with an Alumni Achievement Award. She graduated from UCC with a BSc and HDE in the 1930s, a time when very few women studied science. As a young graduate she worked in UCC's Department of Medicine for 14 years, something Máirín finds remarkable as, initially, she was only employed for that three-week period. The college presented Máirín with a beautiful miniature silver oak tree. 'There's a lovely story about that,' she tells me. 'In 1912, two boys went to Cork city looking for work. One was taken on in a garage, and one was taken on as a gardener in the grounds of UCC. In 1914, they joined the British army and went to the war. In 1918, the garage man, having survived the war, was helping to dig bodies out of the trenches for burial and he dug out his friend, the gardener. And he noticed that there was a little shoot in one of his pockets. So he looked inside, and there were seeds in his pocket, and one of them was growing. So he cut out the pocket and he kept it. Some weeks later, he was in Cork. He went into the grounds of UCC, met the gardener there, and they planted the little seedling down on the banks of the river. It is now a mature oak tree, over 100 years old, and my little oak is a replica.' Fitting too as Máirín herself, at 107, is even older than the oak tree. She is also the proud owner of seven presidential medals, one to mark each year of her life over the centenary.

Máirín has her own recipe for a long, healthy life. 'The secret is everything in moderation. I smoked in college but not for very long. I enjoy my glass of wine, but again in moderation. I had my parents' example. My father liked a bottle of stout, especially when he was doing something like painting a room. Mammy would have the bottle of stout for him when he finished. I would only take a drink on a special occasion, and you appreciate it then. I still like a glass of sherry. I think I prefer sherry to port. And I like a glass of wine with my dinner. I had a glass of wine the other day, it was great. I always have a bottle of sherry in my room and sometimes if I have someone in we'll have a sherry together but the bottle might be there nearly twelve months! I'll tell you a little story. My father and his brother, they were both civil servants. My uncle Rory was particularly good at the high jump and sprinting. In the Gaelic League they used to have all these competitions. Somebody said to Rory, "Do you mind giving me the secret, what do you train on?"

I always have a bottle of sherry in
my room and sometimes if I have
someone in we'll have a sherry
together but the bottle might be
there nearly twelve months!

'"Brown bread and blue duck eggs," he replied.'

And what of death itself? 'And from life to death and what of death itself? You kind of think to yourself, what's it like? You fall asleep, you wake up, and I hope Francis will be there to say, "Welcome." I say my evening prayer and all I hope is that the Lord won't find me wanting, and I ask Our Lady to be with me. Every night I pray that I will be prepared and ready for when He calls me.'

7

The Dooley Family

VISION OF A
UNIFIED NATION

'The Black and Tans went back
into her house and grabbed him
out of the bed in his pyjamas and
threw him into the Blackwater river!
They fired six or seven shots at him;
they missed him but the flood took
him two or three miles down the river.'

Danny Bergin was born in Roscrea on 23 August 1932, one of eight children of Frances Dooley. There were five boys and three girls: 'Mary, Phil, Jimmy, Anne, Francis, Bernadette, Tony and myself.' Danny begins the family story during the War of Independence. 'I had an uncle in Fermoy in Cork, Jim Dooley. He was married to a woman named Maggie. He was very ill with pneumonia, and there was a pub next door. The Black and Tans were around at that time, and they were in the pub, drinking. They were singing and shouting, and so my aunt went into the pub – she wouldn't mince her words now – and told them that she wanted them to quieten down, that her husband was very ill. The next thing anyway, they burst into her house and they grabbed him out of the bed in his pyjamas and threw him into the Blackwater river! There was a big flood at the time. They fired six or seven shots at him; they missed him, but the flood took him two or three miles down the river. He managed to survive but he always maintained that it was his mother who pulled him out of the river. But his mother was dead at the time. Someone found him anyway and took him to the hospital. When they had finished firing at him, they had a can of petrol and they went back to the house and poured the petrol all over it and set fire to the house. That was the sort of thing that happened at the time. He recovered and everything; he went into Cork and set up his own drapery business.

When they had finished firing at
him, they had a can of petrol and
they went back to the house and poured
the petrol all over it and set fire to
the house. That was the sort of thing
that happened at the time.

'I had another uncle, Joe Dooley, a brother of Jim. He was serving his time in the drapery business in Clonmel. He joined the Volunteers in the run-up to 1916. On Holy Thursday, Good Friday he was under orders to be in Dublin. On the Saturday night before the Rising, they marched up to Dublin. They were associated with that.

'Then there was a grand-aunt of mine, back in the early 1900s, an aunt of my mother's, she was a nun. She went to America and then she left the nuns and came back home to Ballinduff in County Galway. She used to tell the story that when she came home one day there were a load of men in what they called the parlour at that time. She didn't know any of them, and what they were doing was trying to put the new Irish constitution together. That would have been a short time before the Rising, maybe 1915 or that. She didn't know who they were but her family's house was a safe house at the time.

'I had another aunt and uncle who lived in another safe house in the foothills of the Slieve Bloom mountains. It was always a safe place for anyone on the run. They would keep them there for two or three days, and if there was any raiding going on, they could disappear into the mountains. That was during the War of Independence. They were very much involved on my mother's side. There was a first

cousin of my mother's who was on the run all the
time. He was a very strong IRA person, a very nice
person, though. Those Dooley safe houses were being
raided all the time. Our own family home wasn't.
They escaped from the worst of it; there weren't any
burnings and they didn't damage the houses. The
burnings were only in the Fermoy area. There were
no real raids around Roscrea, only the burning of
the barracks.

'The Civil War divided a lot of families, mine not
so much. But when the treaty was signed there was
a lot of division. It was an unnecessary war. But any
nation that seeks its independence ends up in a civil
war. The Civil War wouldn't have been very strong
around Roscrea and the surrounding areas, although
there were four young fellas executed in the barracks
in Roscrea alright. I'm not too sure what for. I hate
even thinking about it; it's a thing that should never
have happened. It left the whole country destroyed –
families, relations. I would have liked to see a more
unified nation.'

But when the treaty was signed
there was a lot of division. It was
an unnecessary war. But any nation
that seeks its independence
ends up in a civil war.

Danny's family were farmers. 'We had 60 acres of goodish land, at that time. I was looking at the rent of our place in 1798, 60 acres was 52 pounds and 11 shillings back then. It would have been a lot of money today. It would probably be nearly 300 pounds an acre now, about 345 euro. My father used to grow and sell a lot of potatoes back in 1902. It cost a pound for a tonne of potatoes, and today you'd pay that for just a kilo!

'We think we are in hard times now, and we are in hard times in many ways, but it was very hard in the forties, during the war. We lived well enough though because we had the farm and we lived off the land. And they were big families back then: there were 13 in my maternal great-grandmother's family, and in my mother's family, 11. In my own family there were eight of us and three of us are still alive. My late sister Mary was a historian and worked in the Department of Education for many years; she was involved in compiling the Irish dictionary.'

On 10 August 1966, Danny married his wife, Alice. 'Back in the sixties the weddings would be held at midday. The meal was in a local hotel, they would put up a good meal, and it wouldn't be that expensive. We went down to Kerry for our honeymoon. At that time, we couldn't come home! There weren't that many flats, so we said we would go down to Kerry for a week. And then there were still no flats so we stayed for another week.

'When I think about the cost of setting up home then and now! We furnished our place with a TV and a bed and all, and had ten shillings left out of a hundred pound. At that time you could get a good mahogany bed frame. I don't believe in buying that modern stuff. But Ireland is a strange place, and it is going to be stranger still in another five years. We are going to see changes coming faster and faster.

> But Ireland is a strange place, and it is going to be stranger still in another five years. We are going to see changes coming faster and faster.

'I remember going to school and being in infants and first class. To tell you the truth, when you left national school you had as good an education as you would have in secondary school today. You could basically read and write and count. Today young people have to go to a computer to solve every problem. Back in my day none of us could afford secondary education but you learnt how to live. I worked for what I had, for less than ten pound a week. I worked at everything. I was at home for a good few years and then I worked at building and shearing sheep and that, any way you could make a living. We had a lot more recessions than the one that is coming now: we had a recession in the seventies and in the eighties, and into the nineties. We had to fight our way out of it and build our way up.

'But now I'm listening to all the radio stations and television stations and God is gone out of our lives. Our whole way of life is gone. A husband and wife both have to work now to maintain a home and keep a family. In my time, none of our wives ever worked, and no one can teach a child other than its mother. She is the greatest teacher of all.'

Danny and Alice have four children and nine grandchildren.

Another memory Danny told me about were the country funerals when he was growing up. 'In the countryside back then, when people died the funerals were massive. There would be anywhere up to a thousand people. I remember funerals when I was a child would cost about nine pounds. That would be the undertaker's cost, for bringing them to the church, and the burial, coffin included. You're going back to the thirties and forties, families found it very hard. Fathers wouldn't see the last of their children born: they were dead before then. The churches at that time, you'd see black hats and veils on the women on a Sunday, the church would be full of them. There were three aisles in the church:

there was the men's aisle, the middle aisle, and the women's aisle. The professionals would go down the middle aisle.'

But now I'm listening to all the radio
stations and television stations and God
is gone out of our lives. Our whole way
of life is gone. A husband and wife both
have to work now to maintain a home
and keep a family. In my time, none of
our wives ever worked, and no one can
teach a child other than its mother.
She is the greatest teacher of all.

Now almost 90 years old, Danny reveals his secrets for a long and happy life. 'Get out and about. And I've another secret: go back to simple food. Have porridge in the morning. You go into a supermarket now and there is every sort of a concoction in front of you. All the sort of meats with stuff in them to give it colour and long life and all that. The simple way of life is the best way. People have gone greedy. They want more and more and don't want to work for it anymore. They think they can print money. We have to roll up our sleeves and work hard. A lot of the jobs nowadays are in the financial sector and they spend their day looking at computers and nothing only numbers on them. I would rather spend my life breaking stones. The life you live should be freedom. I wouldn't exchange my life for anything. I had the best of life, the best of people.'

The simple way of life is the best
way. People have gone greedy.
They want more and more and
don't want to work for it anymore.
They think they can print money.

8

The Egans of Croghan

FEIS DAY MEMORIES

*'Seán T. O'Kelly came to the feis and
who accompanied him but uncle Liam!'*

This is the story of the Egan family who lived in the townland of Croghan in north Offaly. They fought in the Civil War and produced a TD, an army chief of staff and a son who studied medicine with Kevin Barry.

For this piece, I spoke to two of their descendants, Margaret Tallon (née Egan) and Martin Mulrennan. But the story begins with their grandparents, Margaret Mulrennan and her brother Patrick. Margaret was married to John Egan and they had five sons and one daughter. The eldest was Liam (born 1896), then John (born 1900), Nicholas (born 1903), Paddy, and Barty, who died in his teens from meningitis, and then their daughter, Mary. John

Senior and his son Liam took a pro-treaty stance during the Civil War, while sons John and Nicholas were both anti-treaty.

'Margaret Egan and my grandfather, Pat Mulrennan, were brother and sister,' Martin Mulrennan tells me. 'The Egans were cousins and neighbours in an adjoining farm in Croghan. They were extensive farmers; their house was Ballyfore House, a large house beside historical Croghan Hill in north Offaly, close to the town of Tyrellspass on the Westmeath side and the town of Daingean on the Offaly side. It's a rural area, the village just had a shop, a church and a school. Very much a rural location.

'As they grew up, the Egan children worked on the family farm, as I did, and they went to the local school at Croghan Hill. Nicholas, John and Liam went to Knockbeg College in Carlow for secondary school. Liam went from there to the seminary in Maynooth. He was

John and Margaret Egan.

in Maynooth until about 1917 or 1918, which would have made him 21 or 22, and he was within six months of being ordained when he left the seminary.'

In 1918, he joined the Dublin Volunteers and from then on he was a career soldier. His niece, Margaret Tallon, recalls that he was 'a very strong, good man, with great integrity. I presume he just thought the priesthood wasn't for him. He was always a religious man, he just didn't have a vocation.'

Liam would have been active during the War of Independence but the change for him came in 1923 when he joined the newly formed Free State army. With his education and military background in the Volunteers, he became an officer. Obviously, joining the Free State army he would have taken the pro-treaty Michael Collins side, and he was an active officer in the Curragh in County Kildare, which was the newly formed military college.

In the meantime, his younger brother John had left Knockbeg in 1918 and went to UCD to study medicine. There he was a classmate of Kevin Barry's, who would be hanged in Mountjoy jail two years later; John and Kevin were the same age and became good friends. 'Recently,' Martin tells me, 'I was looking over a death notice for John in the *Offaly Independent* which appeared in May 1959.'

REGRET IN OFFALY.
THE LATE MR JOHN EGAN

It is with sincere regret we record the death of Mr John Egan, which occurred on Tuesday of last week at a private nursing home in Dublin. The late Mr Egan resided in Ranelagh and was a native of County Offaly. He was the third son of the late Mr and Mrs John Egan, Ballyfore House, Croghan, County Offaly.

As a student in UCD, he was a close personal friend of Kevin Barry. He was a member of the 3rd Battalion, number 1 Offaly Brigade, and later of the 3rd Battalion, Dublin IRA Brigade. He was a brother of Mr Nicholas Egan, County Councillor and TD for the constituency of Laois and County Offaly, and a brother of Major General Liam Egan, Quarter Master General.

John took part in the Dublin Branch of the Volunteers, but when the Civil War situation came, he would have been on the anti-treaty side, like his brother Nicholas, and in complete opposition to his brother Liam who had joined the Irish Free State army.

'Being a close friend of Kevin Barry's,' Martin says, 'he must have been pretty active around Dublin as well. He worked for the Hammond Lane Foundry and in later years he would go around Ireland recovering shipwrecks and that after the war. They were based near Irishtown near the docks, that's where John finished his career.'

The third brother, Nicholas, became TD for Laois–Offaly, first elected in 1954, and re-elected in subsequent elections up until he retired in 1969. He was the youngest brother, born in 1903, and he went to college in Carlow as well.

After leaving school he stayed at home to help out on the family farm. 'So he was the farmer really, and the local politician. Nicholas was active as a young man in the 1919–20 period, before the civil war, and he would have been on the anti-treaty side, de Valera's side, like his brother John. Their father, John senior, was a great Parnell supporter.

Nicholas, standing in front of his father
(father's hands on his shoulders)
and Liam, third from left, back row, with their family. 1915.

'I remember my father saying that during the early days of the conflict, probably in 1922, when Liam joined the Free State army, his brother Nicholas had been arrested and was in prison and Liam went to visit him to bring him some clothes. Apparently an argument ensued and Nicholas threw the clothes back at him through the bars.

'They were incredibly divisive times. I was only a young boy when these gentlemen were alive. I would have been in contact with Nicholas because he had a neighbouring farm to ours in Croghan. He was very much an active Fianna Fáil, de Valera, Seán Lemass supporter throughout his life and active during election times. I remember a particular incident outside the local chapel during election times, when there would have been a skirmish, a lot of heckling and accusations from both sides.

During the early days of the conflict, probably in 1922, when Liam joined the Free State army, his brother Nicholas had been arrested and was in prison and Liam went to visit him to bring him some clothes. Apparently an argument ensued and Nicholas threw the clothes back at him through the bars. They were incredibly divisive times.

'This was in the fifties. I was born in 1952 but I can remember it quite well. There was a lot of animosity in the early days, but then they went on in their different careers. John died in the late twenties and his mother, Margaret, died in 1929. Nicholas remained on the farm, and between that and his work as a county councillor and then a TD, he was a busy man. His wife Sheila (née Creedon) was the local national school teacher and she actually taught me in school.'

Another brother, Patrick, was not involved in the War of Independence or the Civil War but was an enthusiastic Fianna Fáil supporter all his life.

Liam went on to become Army Chief-of-Staff from 1952 to 1955. 'I remember my father telling me that there used to be a famous fleadh, a local feis, beside Croghan Hill back in the forties and fifties. On one particular occasion, the president, who was Seán T. O'Kelly at the time, came to officially open and attend the event, and his accompanier that day was Major Liam T. Egan, the local man.'

Liam's niece Margaret Tallon (née Egan) also remembers that day well. 'We were all very proud of him and the feis in Croghan is one of my nicest memories. We were awfully excited about the feis. It was the 29th of June, St Peter and Paul's feast day. It was very social, you met all your neighbours.

President Eamon de Valera with Liam Egan, Army Chief-of-Staff from 1952–1955.

'Seán T. O'Kelly came to the feis and who accompanied him but Uncle Liam! It was a lovely day. Croghan is only a townland really, and to have the president come and Uncle Liam with him! I would have been 14 or 15 then. It was a big day out, and local people put great work into the feis. We all performed; there were competitions and the local kids performed in them.'

Nicholas continued on farming and being actively involved with Fianna Fáil. He was elected a county councillor in County Offaly, based in Tullamore, and he was very much pro-de Valera. He fought his first election in 1951; he didn't succeed but he was elected in the following election in 1954 and served continuously as a Fianna Fáil TD in Laois–Offaly until 1969. He didn't contest it again in 1969 because he was in poor health and he died the following year.

His daughter, Margaret Tallon, says she always knew her father had been involved in the Civil War. 'He was born in 1903, so he was quite young. I remember hearing that he was in jail. He was in Mountjoy. That was before he had children, he didn't get married until 1937 and he was a farmer after that. He was involved as a young man, evidently, or he wouldn't have been in jail. He was in jail with Seán MacBride. He was a sociable, kind man with a great sense of humour.

'We were very conscious of having a TD as a dad. I know people give out about TDs but they work terribly hard. He was always working; he had plenty of help on the farm.

'I remember typing letters for him, though. He was away a lot and we were very conscious of that. And people were coming to him to sort out their problems. We went to the local primary school, and it wasn't spoken about much. My mother was the local teacher.

'My father was very keen on developing employment. There were turf bogs around our area. There was very little employment in Croghan at that time, and then Bord na Móna started. My father was always helping people before he was ever a TD, he was on so many committees. And he helped the local people a lot, they came to him a lot. It was mainly help with employment. He was a TD for 15 years, 1954 to 1969. He was quite young when he died at the age of 67. He had a stroke. He worked so hard, he would have been re-elected in the next general election.'

Nicholas and his brother Liam became close after the Civil War. 'When Daddy would go to the Dáil, he would stay overnight with uncle Liam in Rathfarnham. They are all dead now, but uncle Liam and my father ended up great friends and he depended on uncle Liam a lot. Everything ended up as one happy family, and my father would always speak very kindly of his own father: there was no bitterness there.'

Uncle Liam married twice. In his first marriage to Nonie Spain he had three daughters and a son. Tragically his son was drowned as a child. After Nonie died Liam married again, Mary O'Flaherty, and they had one little daughter who died as a baby. The fourth brother, Paddy, settled as a farmer in Broadford in County Kildare, and he died in 1979. Martin says, 'I remember it was the year the Pope came to Ireland.' Paddy married and had seven children.

The Egans had one sister, Mary. Born in 1895, she was the eldest, and worked as a priest's housekeeper.

Mary never married, and she died of typhoid in 1937 when she was only 42 years old. John married late in life and was very happy.

Nicholas had seven children: Margaret, Kathleen, Sheila, Grace, Mary, Bríd and Johnny. 'My mother, Sheila, was very busy, but she had help. She died in November 1990. She was a good age, 85.'

Margaret tells a story about her family which epitomises the tragedy of the War of Independence and the Civil War where families were often split by the stance they took on the Treaty. 'My father's first cousin, Joe Byrne, was executed by the Free State during the Civil War. When Joe's sister, Mary Byrne, and Liam Egan (pro-Treaty) met afterwards at a family funeral they just approached each other and put their arms around each other. It was a lovely symbol of reconciliation and showed there was no bitterness among the family.'

9

Martin Meleady

THE CHE GUEVARA
OF TULLAMORE

'Thank God they didn't search the
hay rick because your father had
bullets in the hay rick!'

'**M**y grandfather, Martin Meleady, was
continuously on the run for three or four
years, he was kind of the Che Guevara of the
Tullamore area! He had a nickname locally – Poirín
– that would be a term that was used to refer to
small spuds or small items. He was small in stature,
5 feet 8 inches, but he was a tough scrapper.'

I'm chatting with Martin's grandson, Martin
Mulrennan. Born in 1895, his grandfather came
from a family of six girls and two boys. 'From a

Martin Meleady in uniform, c.1916.

very young age he was very active with the IRB, which morphed into the IRA. He was imprisoned in Portlaoise in 1916, initially by the British, because of his activities. At a later date he was imprisoned in Scotland. His main activity was that he was the quarter-master of the local branch of the Offaly Brigade, based in Tullamore. He was quite important. His main function was to store the weapons and ammunition and bomb-making equipment.'

Martin's brother James was a blacksmith. 'He wasn't quite as active in the movement, but being a blacksmith, he would have been preparing what they euphemistically called "stuff". That usually involved improvised explosive devices and handmade bullets and stuff like that. He had six sisters, and at least three of them were in Cumann na mBan. They subsequently applied for Cumann na mBan pensions. The other sisters subsequently joined the Holy Faith order in Glasnevin as nuns. Religion and politics were very popular in our family. It is a lethal mix! Two of them were teachers and one of them was a nurse. Their names were Sr Martha, Sr Mobhi and Sr John. They were teaching in Holy Faith schools around Dublin city mainly. The three older sisters married and their married names were Mrs Elizabeth Ward, Mrs Treacy and Mrs Teresa O'Brien – Teresa was a common name in the Meleadys, the same name as my mother and grandmother. Their main function in Cumann na mBan was to have the so-called Meleady "safe house" available to IRA Volunteers on the run, prepare meals and takeaway food and to carry messages and weapons on their bikes to the surrounding areas of Tullamore, Clara, Kilbeggan, Ballycommon and Killeigh, a radius of about ten miles from their home.

'They would carry messages, and my mother used to say that on a fair day, which was always a Friday, they would be going into town, and the farmers' wives or daughters would bring in homemade butter or eggs or poultry into the local shops, in exchange for the usual goods – tea, sugar, necessities. Most families were sort of self-sufficient then. When they were bringing their messages into town, they would have them wrapped up on their person. These would be messages to the local IRA commanders. They would have been stopped on a number of occasions, but usually the Black and Tans were reluctant to search girls, particularly younger girls, so they were used for that purpose. I'm not sure if any of them carried guns, but they would certainly have had access to arms, because their brother Martin was the quartermaster of the local Tullamore IRA brigade. Guns and equipment were regularly stored in the farmyard and surrounding buildings and land.

> When they were bringing their messages into town, they would have them wrapped up on their person. These would be messages to the local IRA commanders. They would have been stopped on a number of occasions, but usually the Black and Tans were reluctant to search girls, particularly younger girls, so they were used for that purpose.

'James had to look after both the forge and the family farm, because Martin was continuously on the run. Then there were the prisons. Martin was in five or six prisons in total, including Tullamore prison where there was an attempt to rescue him. There was a sum of one hundred pounds raised by the local brigade to influence the prison guards. But the night before he was due to be sprung he was transferred to Portlaoise. He also served time in the Curragh holding centre, Ballykinlar internment camp, Kilmainham, Belfast and the Curragh internment camp where his involvement in an attempt to burn the prison saw him sentenced to 18 months' hard labour in Perth jail in Scotland.

'In 1921 he was released from Perth jail and he travelled home on a steam ship. But that was shipwrecked, so he floated in to the North Wall in Dublin on a plank! He had escaped from a number of prisons so that's why he had been sent to the high-security facility in Scotland. He was considered a dangerous man, I suppose.'

Martin Meleady's grand-nephew, John McDonald, wrote an account of the shipwreck in the 2017 *Tullamore Annual*. This is an extract:

Back row, Sr Martha, Sr Mobhi and Sr John. Sr Antoine, Martin's daughter, in front. All Holy Faith sisters, Carysfort Training College, Dublin, 1966.

Martin was released from Perth jail on October 22nd 1921 and boarded the Laird Line SS *Rowan* at Greenock, Glasgow with nothing but the clothes he wore on his back as he prepared to journey back to Ireland. As the SS *Rowan* was steaming out of harbour, a disaster was about to unfold. The *Rowan*, for some inexplicable reason, collided with the steamer *Belfast*. Perhaps it was the thick fog that enveloped the harbour that was the primary cause of the collision. There was utter panic and confusion on board the *Rowan* in the immediate aftermath of impact. The collision was so severe that the *Rowan* keeled over almost immediately.

Martin knew he was in mortal danger as he clawed his way up the tiled decks. Most of the seventy to eighty passengers who had been on board were still clinging to the rails. Suddenly another ship loomed out of the fog. It was an American steamer coming to their rescue but it cut through the *Rowan* in the poor visibility, sending it straight to the bottom.

Martin remembered being tangled in ropes that hung from the side of the *Rowan*.

'Martin was greatly influenced by his mother Teresa, my great-grandmother, who was left a widow with eight young children. She had a great interest in the Irish preoccupation with land, because her own father, Martin Flanagan, had been evicted from his homestead outside Tullamore, near the village of Killeigh. I recall my mother telling me about doing an article some time in primary school about famous Irish figures and she chose Parnell. She often repeated her grandmother's words, "I saw Parnell in Tullamore." There had been a mass gathering in Tullamore and Parnell came down on the train. Teresa was born in 1864, so Parnell would have been at his height and she would have been a young girl who went along to this meeting about land reform. Teresa was certainly actively involved with the land agitation movement and was very much influenced by her father and the fact that he had been evicted. We also have to remember that her father lived through the Great Famine. Teresa lived to be 90. I went to her funeral as a young boy.

'My mother Teresa married Patrick Mulrennan. Patrick is the son of Pat, who was the brother of Margaret Egan Senior. 'That's how I became a Mulrennan. I have two brothers and two sisters: Mary, Carmel, Pat and Ray. We're keeping the name "Pat" going: my son is Shane Patrick and he would be the fifth Mulrennan.'

Teresa only passed away in February 2021. 'She had dementia but her long-term memory was brilliant – she could remember back to her first holy communion in 1937. She also remembered her boarding school days in a convent in Mountmellick where she said she often went to bed hungry at night. My father died in 1986; he was 69.'

It was only in his last year that his grandfather spoke about any of this. 'He was a man of very few words but maybe after a few pints you might get a story out of him. On one occasion, he told me he'd been very much a wanted man, there were spies and whatever in the area. He was after carrying out a raid, raiding an RIC party that were escorting TNT. There were a few quarries around Tullamore, and explosives would be sent down to the local train station and escorted by the RIC to the quarries in Tullamore, Kilbeggan and Clara. My grandfather's mission was to ambush the escort, to take the RIC's weapons; they carried Webley revolvers, and they usually had spare ammunition. They would take that, and the explosives that were being used for the quarry, and use them to make bombs. Because of his activities, he had to go on the run very frequently, mainly, he told me, into the Slieve Bloom mountains. He would hide out in the mountains on the Laois–Offaly border, around the villages of Clonaslee and Rosenallis.

'It was while on the run that he met his future wife and my grandmother, Mary Dunne. He met her initially in Portlaoise prison. She was a young girl, a teenager; she was born in 1905 so she would have been going to school at the time. She came from Clonabeg, Clonaslee, County Laois. She was going to the local school, and her teachers organised some of her classmates to knit some scarves and jumpers for the prisoners in Portlaoise. So she was about 15 years old then and she first met my grandfather in the prison.

'Then, some years later, my grandfather was hiding out in Mary's family house, which was one of the safe houses; he stayed there occasionally, but never more than a night or two because they had to move continuously. In the meantime, when he was on the run, his mother, who was a widowed woman, was trying to keep the family farm going and his six sisters and brothers!

'One day in 1920 the Black and Tans arrived at the Meleady family farm. My grandfather was in prison in Scotland at the time. They arrived in two or three tenders, a couple of dozen soldiers, well-armed. They knocked on the door, and my grandmother answered. They said they were looking for her son and she told them, "I don't know where he is, he hasn't been here recently." The officer in charge said, "We know your son is involved in the IRA and we have information that he has been storing arms. We are going to search your house, tear it asunder, and then we are going to search the farmyard. If we happen to find anything, we are going to burn this house down, so get ready to leave!"

'She told them that she was a poor widow woman and the children were very young. But that didn't stop the Black and Tans. They raided the house, a long, thatched house with settle beds and a loft. They searched the house, turned everything upside down, ransacked it and searched the thatch with their bayonets. When they couldn't find anything there they went round all the sheds where the livestock were, and around the hay rick, and the straw rick down near the orchard, didn't look into them with the bayonets but went right around them looking for anything inside. They couldn't find anything so they left, but they warned her they would return later.

'My grandmother told my mother, "Thank God they didn't search the hay rick because your father had bullets in the hay rick!" When he wasn't in prison, my grandfather was continually on the run in the Slieve Bloom mountains! He lived to the age of 95 and I remember one night over a couple of pints trying to get some information out of him.

"Can you recall any particular incident when you felt like your life was in danger?" I asked him.

And he replied, "I was in danger on many occasions, literally running from houses and bullets, but one thing that stands out in my mind is the raid on the pub in Ballycommon."

'Now there's a pub on the bridge in the townland of Ballycommon, four miles from Tullamore, quite close to his homestead. They were preparing an ambush, him and a few comrades, for a regular Black and Tan tender that would pass through the area at a given time each day. They were on the roof of the pub, with their rifles, ready to ambush the tender, kill the soldiers and take the arms. They were expecting one tender, an armoured car, carrying six, eight or ten soldiers, but they got a huge shock when a second car arrived. They would have been outnumbered. When the first armoured car drove past, they opened fire on them. The British army returned fire, and when they saw the second car coming they had to lie low on the roof because there was fire coming from the second car as well, and one thing my grandfather said was, "I can remember vividly wearing a pair of hobnailed boots, boots with studs and a steel cap on the heel. There was a huge amount of fire coming from the Black and Tans, and we were trying to get the odd shot in, and at one point the fire was so intense, I just had to keep my head buried down and lie on my stomach. The only thing sticking up was the two heels of my hobnailed boots." He said that they were obviously very good shots – the only thing they could see glaring in the sun was his steel-capped boots, so they shot the two heels off his boots! I asked him what he did then, and he said, "I just ran for it, we scattered into the bog!" They didn't kill him, just left him shoeless! I remember as young fellas going to school, some of my friends wore those boots. They would have been made by cobblers, studs on them and the heel was like a horseshoe.'

I can remember vividly wearing a pair of hobnailed boots, boots with studs and a steel cap on the heel. There was a huge amount of fire coming from the Black and Tans, and we were trying to get the odd shot in, and at one point the fire was so intense, I just had to keep my head buried down and lie on my stomach. The only thing sticking up was the two heels of my hobnailed boots.

But, according to Martin, those who took part in the Civil War in the area have been reluctant to talk about it. 'I was down in Tullamore a couple of years ago and I called to the old former Meleady homestead, where my mother was born. It is now a dilapidated thatched house. I met a neighbour there: his father was a comrade of my grandfather, and he would have been a commanding officer of the Tullamore brigade. I also met his son who was in an adjoining homestead. He came to have a look around and we had a chat and I told him who I was, and of course he knew my grandfather's name, Martin Meleady. I asked the neighbour if his father spoke much about it and he said, "Very little." I got the distinct impression from him that, as an old man, his father was very saddened and disillusioned by the whole episode, the Civil War that achieved nothing.

'My grandfather moved from his farm in Tullamore to Croghan near the Egan family in 1936 when my mother was only six. And, lo and behold, who should his neighbouring farmer be on one side than a former Free State army officer, Captain John Rigney, who would have been his sworn enemy during the Civil War. It wasn't that long afterwards really! Actually Captain John Rigney's farm was between the Egan and Meleady farms. I asked my grandfather if they got on and he said that the day they arrived, he remembers this man coming and introducing himself, welcoming my grandfather to the area and saying, "Lookit, we both fought in the war, let's let bygones be bygones, we're now neighbours, let us go in peace now."'

Martin Meleady left Croghan in 1960, sold the farm and moved to the village of Clonbullogue near Edenderry. He continued farming there right up to his eighties and he died in 1990. 'He was a man of few words. I remember one time, it was a fair day in Tyrellspass around 1959. I can remember it well because it was the year I made my first communion.

Martin Meleady
outside his home in
Clonbullogue, Edenderry,
County Offaly, c.1980s.

That time you would walk the livestock from the farm to the local fair day. The boys of the house would be brought along to stand in the gaps and the gates to help herd the livestock. You would meet up with neighbours along the way and go in a convoy and little boys would run ahead to bring the livestock into the fair. The fair would be on every month.

'I remember one particular incident where my father was bringing cattle along with my grandfather. At the end of the day when the cattle had been sold and money exchanged – it was all cash then – they went to the local pub. Martin Moore's pub in Tyrellspass. They had a couple of drinks and I had my red lemonade. As the night progressed, my grandfather got into an argument with an old adversary. There were some heated words exchanged, and the owner of the bar, the owner's daughter actually, asked them to leave. It continued on bitterly, a scrap, in the pub yard. As a seven-year-old, I was shocked and not quite sure what was going on! I do remember various exchanges taking place. I don't recall the man's name who he was fighting but it was obviously political.

'I remember working alongside him on the farm. I would have got up as a young boy at five and six o'clock in the morning, milked the cows, fed the pigs, and then I'd go and serve half seven mass! After that I'd go home and have breakfast and walk three miles to school!

'At the outbreak of hostilities in Northern Ireland in the late 1960s, Martin was approached by the Provisional IRA to see if he would "assist in the cause", but he said, "Lads, I'm an old man, my war is over." At that stage he was in his mid-seventies. I think they wanted him to store some "stuff"; they knew about his history. I got the impression he was disillusioned. The anti-treaty side were hardliners: de Valera walked out of the Dáil and wouldn't agree to a treaty on the grounds that the country was going to be divided.'

10

Michael Feerick

ON HORSEBACK
THROUGH THE TOWN

'Michael rode his white horse through the
streets of Dunmore shouting at the Black
and Tans, calling them "blackguards".'

'**M**ichael Feerick, my maternal grandfather, emigrated to America during the time before the Free State was born.' I'm chatting to Frank Gannon, Michael Feerick's 82-year-old grandson. 'My grandparents met in New York. My grandmother, Delia McDonagh, was a personal nanny to the Rockefeller kids. She was a nanny and a very good cook, and she was with them for years. She had to have a bit of class working for them! They had a place way upstate by the lakes. They

Michael and Delia, with two of their children, Tootsie and Dan, c.1923.

went up there during the summer when the kids were off school, for six or seven weeks. They had a great life. Delia was one of the family really and was treated that way. She reckoned the Rockefeller kids had more of an Irish accent than an American one because of her! John Rockefeller was very proud of that fact. I think there were three children.

'Everyone went to America at 18 or 19 back then, anyone could go. They all went around the turn of the century. What happened was someone would go and make money and send back the money for the passage of the next one. Michael's sister was called Mary; she went out first. She never married or anything, but she made a lot of money and sent it back to the rest of them. I'm not sure where exactly my grandfather met Delia, probably at a dance hall or a bar or in Central Park.

'Michael came from Knockatee and he kept two saloons in New York for a while and then, when prohibition came in, he went driving the trams. That was the last job he had, driving the trams in New York. He was a staunch supporter of de Valera, a staunch supporter of the Rising, really, because Michael Collins and de Valera fought together for a long time; that separation only happened later. He donated a lot of money to their cause. He sent two thousand dollars home to Ireland to help set up the banking system. When Ireland broke away from Britain and got freedom, after the treaty was signed, they had to set up some sort of a banking system. A lot of people all over the world who had money sent it home to set up the first Central Bank of Ireland.

'Michael and Delia got married in New York in St Patrick's Cathedral, right across the road from the Rockefeller Centre. I don't know if the Rockefellers went to the wedding, but they gave them a house on 52nd, between Fifth Avenue and Lexington Avenue, which would be a very high-class area. I don't think they gave them the title of the house, but they had a rent-free house to live in. They were lucky, but they worked for it.

Mick Feerick, cutting turf on the farm.

'It broke my grandmother's heart to come back to Ireland, but they had to come home to look after the farm after Michael's father died. She loved New York. My grandmother died when I was 9 or 10, but my grandfather told me plenty of stories about New York. He always wanted me to go there. He used to say, "Why are you going back to that rotten country?" meaning England. He hated it. I loved England, I really loved it. He was delighted when I went to America, but he died while I was over there. He was 89 or something – he lived to be a big age. We got on very well together, we were very close.

'He loved whiskey. He would go to town four times a week, every other day into Dunmore. He didn't like beer; he would buy one beer and leave it over to the side and start into the whiskey.

'When Michael came home to Ireland, there were no cars to rent, so he bought a big white horse and a saddle. He was a big fella, 6 feet 3 inches, and he always wore a hat. He was in Dunmore one evening having a few drinks and getting quite "steamed up". The Black and Tans were also out causing trouble, abusing the barmen and refusing to pay for their drinks. So Michael rode his white horse through the streets of Dunmore shouting at the Black and Tans, calling them "blackguards", a very old-fashioned terminology for "thieves". and he was also shouting, "Go back to England, you suckers, you're over here terrorising the people of Ireland." Michael had been in America for a long time and had an American accent. The Black and Tans retaliated by aiming their guns at him on his white horse. Then the captain of the Black and Tans gave the order, "Don't fire. He's a Yank!" All these 'Tans were cocking their guns, you could hear the *click, click, click,* and the officer in charge was screaming at them, "Do not fire, do not fire. He's a Yank!" Because he had an American accent, you see, they thought he *was* American. It would have been outrageous to shoot an American at that time. Other than that, they would have shot him dead.

> It would have been outrageous to shoot an American at that time. Other than that, they would have shot him dead.

'Michael came to Ireland a few times before he finally came to settle here altogether. I think he came after the Great Depression, after the banking system broke down in 1929. He was farming cattle, he had a bit of money. He had three children; two of them were born in America, Danny and Nora, and then Lily was born in Knockatee. Nora was my mother, but they all called her Tootsie, for some reason or another. My grandfather had a farm with a bull. He traded in cattle – he used to go round all the markets and sell a few cattle and beets and potatoes and that. Everybody killed a pig at the time, so you'd have your own rashers and sausages and bacon and all that. I remember going to the mill with my grandfather. Every farmhouse had a big bag of flour in a recess beside the fireplace, a ten-stone bag of flour and a bag of oatmeal. What you'd do is take two bags to the mill, and you would call back for it two days later and you'd have your oatmeal. It was pinhead oatmeal, it had a lot of oat flour in it, and made marvellous bread and wonderful porridge, a different type of porridge altogether.'

Frank himself was born on 4 May 1939 in Birmingham in England. 'My mother was Irish-American. Her mother was from Mayo, and my father was from Clonbern. They met in Birmingham; they were working there because there was no

Frank Gannon.

work in Ireland. My mother came home from America when she was about ten. Her father had inherited a small farm of land in Knockatee.

'My parents got married in Birmingham before the war broke out. I was born there the year before the Germans bombed Birmingham – our house got damaged with the bombs. Myself and my mother and my sister Mary, she was three at the time, I was about one, and we had to go out to the air raid shelter in the back garden. One night there was a big bomb with a whistle on it, like a siren, when it came down, to frighten the people. My father went to look and see where it was going to fall, and the door got blown right open and blew the windows open and there was glass everywhere. After that my parents took me and my sister home to our grandparents in Knockatee for safe keeping and left us there. They went back to England. My father was in the war effort building shelters and my mother was working in a munitions factory.

One night there was a big bomb with a
whistle on it, like a siren, when it came
down, to frighten the people. My father
went to look and see where it was going
to fall, and the door got blown right open
and blew the windows open and there
was glass everywhere.

'I have three brothers and two sisters. They were big families back then. I am the eldest, then Mary, John, Kathleen, Freddie and James. Mary and I were brought up in Ireland; we lived with my grandparents while my parents were in Birmingham. We didn't see my parents for three years – I didn't know them when they came back! They had two more children shortly after coming home, and then there was a big break of nine years and they had two more! They thought they were safe, I think!

'I loved living with my grandparents. I have the happiest memories of growing up in Knockatee, a little thatched house with not much room – for a while we slept in the bed with my grandmother and then she got us a little cot. I think I was one end of the cot and Mary was the other end. It was a lovely farm; I was really happy. I was very unhappy when my parents came home, and I had to go to Clonbern! They were complete strangers to me then.

'Going to school at that time wasn't fun. Everybody got the cane, every day, for nothing. Brought down on your knuckles, they would be jailed if it was done today.

'I spent a large chunk of my own life abroad, 13 years working in England and then 18 years in New York; the rest of the time I was at home. But the years in England were the happiest of my life, I think the sun shone for the first time on me when I went back to Birmingham. I worked in construction, first of all as a labourer, working with bricklayers, carrying bricks and mortar up to them. Then I got to know how to use the trowel, and I started to pick it up myself; it was a bit of an apprenticeship. I was 17 when I moved to Birmingham. I was 45 when I went to America. I couldn't get work anywhere here, and because I had been a bricklayer and a subcontractor, I couldn't get the dole or anything.

'I thought about going back to England, but I couldn't face it. So then I thought I would go to New York, and I had no problem with that because my mother was an American citizen. I got a green card straight away. I had a good trade as a stonemason and a bricklayer, and I got the best work. If I could earn 200 or 300 pounds a week, I wouldn't have left Ireland, but over there I was getting 2,000 dollars a week.

If I could earn 200 or 300 pounds
a week, I wouldn't have left Ireland,
but over there I was getting
2,000 dollars a week.

'One day I was talking to a man in New York, he was saying he couldn't get any bricklayers to build a chimney. He'd got a price off a man for 4,000 dollars for the job, and I said, "By God, I'll do it for five hundred."

He said, "If you can come to New York, I will put you up and I'll give you 4,000 dollars for building a chimney." So I went. There was work everywhere and he still said he couldn't find anyone to build the chimney. He met me at the station and insisted on giving me the 4,000 dollars, and all of a sudden I had a lot of money!

'Then everyone on that street wanted me to do something for them. New sidewalks and walls and chimneys and everything. I couldn't get out of that street! It was all cash too.

'My wife was Marie Tuite from County Meath. I met her at a dancehall in Birmingham. She was at home in Ireland while I was over in the States for the first few months and she said she would come over for a holiday. I said, "Marie, bring whatever you can with you and close up the house." We had a daughter at the time who was 14, so she had to finish off her schooling in the States. Two different systems of education. This is Mary Lisa. I have three children, one boy and two girls. Michael is the eldest, Caroline is next, and Mary Lisa is the youngest.

'I stayed in the States for 18 years. I came home because of my wife's health – she was suffering from Parkinson's. She lived to be 79 and spent the last four years of her life in Central Park nursing home in Clonbern which is owned by my daughter, Caroline. The name of the nursing home is a tribute to all the years the family spent in New York. Marie and I had a good long life together; we were 55 years married when she died.'

Frank has four grandchildren and two great-grand-children and he is very proud of his grandfather. 'Hearing stories about him makes my heart jump. He was my hero. I first started hearing these stories when I was 9 or 10. I lived with him from when I was one year old, I was very close to him. I think of him all the time, and I visit his grave in Dunmore, on the top of the hill at the highest point.'

11

Alice Quinn

WARTIME BRIDE AND WIDOW

'There was a knock on the door at about 9 p.m. and a man who was obviously the commanding officer of a battalion of Black and Tans said that he had 14 men who were hungry and needed feeding!'

On the eve of the First World War, 22-year-old Alice Quinn met and fell in love with Charlie Chambers, a young soldier who had just joined the British army. Alice's granddaughter, Cathy Cregan, tells me about her grandmother's whirlwind romance. 'They fell in love and got married much quicker than they would have ordinarily, and he went off to fight. Alice wrote to him, she wrote endless letters, and he wrote back to her too. He had a friend in the trenches in France, and he used to read his letters from Alice to this friend. Sadly, Charles was killed in 1916 at the Battle of the Somme and was buried in a military cemetery in France. Afterwards, Charlie's friend came to see Nana when he came back from the war. He told her that *he* had fallen in love with her through her letters! But Alice wasn't interested in him.

'They fell in love and got married much quicker than they would have ordinarily, and he went off to fight. Alice wrote to him, she wrote endless letters, and he wrote back to her too. He had a friend in the trenches in France, and he used to read his letters from Alice to this friend. Sadly, Charles was killed in 1916 at the Battle of the Somme and was buried in a military cemetery in France.

'Nobody knew that Nana had married back then; she never spoke about it and we only found out after she died in 1970 when her sister told us. But Nana wore that wedding ring all her life on a chain around her neck. After Charlie she went on to marry my grandfather and have seven children. Noel was the eldest, and then my father Richard, but everyone called him Reg. Then there was Paddy, Paul, Ronald, Betty and Harry. Only one girl, poor auntie Betty, in the middle of all that!

'My grandfather was Patrick Cregan, but known to everyone as "Bruddy", because he had a little sister who couldn't say Patrick when she was small, so she called him her big bruddy! So he was always known as Bruddy Cregan. He was an ambitious man for the time, I think. He decided that he wanted to be a bookmaker on the racecourse, and he made quite a bit of money along the way. I think he was also left some money by his family. He went on to buy an office in Fairview for his bookmaking business. So he had on-course bookmaking and this big office in Fairview.

'He was originally from Galway, and Nana was a Dub. She married Bruddy and they bought a house in Fairview, a little red-brick house, and started their family. It was a small enough house, but Bruddy was doing well financially, the family was growing, and next thing they bought a house in Kenilworth Square. My father has some memory of being in Fairview, but I think most of his childhood memories were in Kenilworth Square. They became a well-to-do family, in that Nana had a cook and a scullery maid, all of whom lived in the house. My grandfather never drove, but he had a car, and he had a driver called Martin who also did the garden. It was a very posh

Alice in the garden of her house on Kenilworth Square.
Alice was always feeling sorry for people and taking them in.
The two Japanese men had been in Clongowes when
the war broke out. They couldn't get home and so
moved in with the family for the duration.

household. Most of the boys were sent to Clongowes Wood College as boarders.

'Alice was very traditional in many ways: a great cook, a lover of children, a great person for encouraging and telling children they were great, even if they weren't. She started life in Golden Lane, in a house along there. She was a seamstress and she had sisters – I knew one sister, Annie. Her father worked with trains, I believe. She worked as a seamstress from when she left school, and her sister Annie worked with her. They made dresses for all the rich people back then.

'When the family was living in Fairview everyone

was terrified of the Black and Tans. They had just landed in Dublin and had the reputation of being total scoundrels. On one particular occasion, Nana was at home; she was expecting a baby. Noel and my father were small children then. Bruddy was at the races somewhere. There was a knock on the door at about 9 p.m. and a man who was obviously the commanding officer of a battalion of Black and Tans said that he had 14 men who were hungry and needed feeding!

'Auntie Annie was there too as Nana didn't like being alone at night when Bruddy was away. All of the women were terrified of the Black and Tans. So there was this knock at the door, and 14 men to be fed. Nana didn't know what to do, she hadn't that much food in the house, she had probably fed everyone in the family already that day. She said they were an awful mob, and if you didn't know better, you would feel sorry for them. They didn't really have proper uniforms, and the clothes they *did* have were rough – you would give them tuppence on the street, they looked so poverty-stricken, she said. They were all very skinny and foul-smelling, as if they hadn't washed in a long, long time. Nana had very little in the house, but she had bread and potatoes, and I think some rashers, sausages and eggs. She had some leftover soup as well, because herself and Bruddy used to make soup every day in case Bruddy had some of his friends over. Some of the days he wasn't working he would go out for a few drinks and bring back his drinking buddies and have some hot kidney soup, and they would play poker into the small hours of the morning.

'So Nana cooked up whatever she had in the house and the men sat around in the street and on walls until the food was ready. She had no idea why her house was picked out; there was no particular reason why they came to her house, but they did. She was very shaken by the experience and said she nearly had to be revived with smelling salts afterwards! She was very shook and so was Annie. But to be fair to the men, she said they were quite mannerly and thanked her for the food, and cleared up the plates, even though they were so feared and had such terrible reputations. They simply sat there and filled their faces, drank several pots of tea and headed off. She had to do two sittings because she hadn't that many plates.

But to be fair to the men, she said they
were quite mannerly and thanked her
for the food, and cleared up the plates,
even though they were so feared and had
such terrible reputations. They simply sat
there and filled their faces, drank several
pots of tea and headed off.

'They were out of there by midnight, and Bruddy came home not long after that, probably three sheets to the wind, and didn't believe her. But it was true, and she was very shaken by it, to the point that she was afraid to answer the door unless she was expecting someone.

When they moved to Kenilworth Square in Rathgar, life got much easier for Nana. She loved having her pals in for afternoon tea and all that. My father used to tell great stories about life there. He loved nothing more than to make my mother's life hell, and the cook's life hell, and anyone else he could manage! He would play jokes and tricks.

'Nana had her friends in one afternoon, and the cat was about to have kittens. So he arrives into this group of ladies who are sitting there in their beautiful frocks having cucumber sandwiches, and he says, "Mum, I think the cat is about to have kittens, but don't worry, I have it under control." He arrives back in about ten minutes later with tomato ketchup squeezed all over rubber gloves and says, "I'm doing a caesarean!" And all the women fainted and had to be revived! Always some shenanigans going on in Kenilworth Square, with parties and piano-playing and all that. They had a gay old time.

'My grandfather was only 49 when he died. He

had a lovely life, playing golf out in Hermitage. Martin would drive him out and wait for him. Grandad would linger at the nineteenth hole for quite some time – I think that's probably why he didn't drive the car!

'The whole family would pack up for the summer, and take a house in Skerries – the whole family, and the cook and scullery maid and everything. It was like Downton Abbey! My dad was born in 1924, so I think he was around six or seven when they were doing stuff like that. He started off in one of those little schools and he was expelled from three schools by the time he was six! He was an awful scoundrel. He started mitching almost as soon as he started school, up the back lanes on his own. He said a man came along one day and he asked the man what time it was, but this man must have been wise to what Reg was doing, and he said, "It's ten to one, you better get home to your mother for lunch", and Reg arrived home to find out it was only a quarter past ten, so he was caught red-handed! Another school he was sent to, they had a raffle. He loved raffles, thought they were a great lark altogether, but he was overly ambitious and entered himself into the raffle and came first, second and third, so he was expelled from that school as well!

The whole family would pack up for the
summer, and take a house in Skerries – the
whole family, and the cook and scullery maid
and everything. It was like Downton Abbey!

'Reg used to be in the local sweet shop in Harold's
Cross quite regularly, and he met this Jewish fellow
who asked him would he like to do some work for
him, as in going round to all the Jewish houses in
the neighbourhood, lighting the fires on a Friday
night. There were quite a few Jewish families in
the neighbourhood at that time, and they weren't
allowed light the fire on the Sabbath, so that's what
Dad got his money from! He was only eight when he
started that. The man who took him on to do it was
only a few years older than him, but he was Chaim
Herzog, who went on to become President of Israel!

He met this Jewish fellow who asked him
would he like to do some work for him, as
in going round to all the Jewish houses
in the neighbourhood, lighting the fires
on a Friday night. There were quite a few
Jewish families in the neighbourhood at
that time, and they weren't allowed light
the fire on the Sabbath.

'Then Dad went to St Mary's in Rathmines, and I think he was quite young being sent to Clongowes, maybe about 11. He loved it, though, he absolutely loved it. He said they were the best years of his life.

'He wanted to be a doctor, but sadly Bruddy, possibly through his lifestyle of staying up late and drinking and all that, got pancreatic cancer at 49, which was really, really sad. Nana was left with seven children then. Noel was the eldest. He had just left Clongowes and had to take over the bookie business, and he hated it. He absolutely hated it. He wasn't very good at it either – they were losing money hand over fist. Because Dad used to help his father out on the racecourse, he knew more about it than Noel did, so he had no choice but to be taken out of Clongowes and put into the family business full time, to keep the roof over his family's head. It was awful because his dream never came true. He was able to do the job, but it wasn't his first love: that was to become a doctor. He stayed with the job his whole life because that was all he knew, really.

'There was one point later where foot and mouth was threatening the bookies, every business really, anything to do with animals. My mum and dad opened a restaurant then, for a couple of years. It was called Le Petit and it was popular with Charlie Haughey and all the politicians and theatre people.

Mum and Dad sold it to the man who is the owner of Taj Mahal now. Mum is convinced that the gun-running was planned in her place!

'Nana was left a widow at a young age, but she managed. They had to sell the house in Kenilworth Square at some point. By then Noel was married, Betty was married. Betty got married very young, only 17 or 18. I have more cousins than you could shake a stick at. They adored my father; he was the most beloved of all the uncles. He had dementia for more than ten years. Realistically, from about 2000 to when he died in 2013.

I looked after him for several years at home, and he spent the last four years in a nursing home in Bray.

Alice, in the dark suit with the feather
in her hat, at her daughter's wedding.

'Where the family courts are now, Dolphin House, it's the site of what used to be the Dolphin hotel, which was a very popular place in Dublin, and my grandfather Bruddy drank in there most evenings when he was in town. He used to wait for the clock to strike six o'clock, the bells of the Angelus were pealing all around Dublin, and as soon as that stopped, he would turn around in the bar and say, "What are you all having?" In fact, that was his nickname: he was known as "What are you all having?" No wonder money went out the window!

'One of his drinking buddies, who he drank with quite a bit, was Michael Collins. He wasn't a close friend or anything, but he definitely used to have a few drinks with him in the Dolphin hotel when they were both young men.

> One of his drinking buddies, who he drank with quite a bit, was Michael Collins. He wasn't a close friend or anything, but he definitely used to have a few drinks with him in the Dolphin hotel when they were both young men.

'Nana ended up living with her daughter Betty for many years. Betty was married to a man called Aidan McNally, who had been a student in Clongowes with Dad. Dad brought Aidan home. Aidan was from Newry, and he came with Dad to Kenilworth Square for the summer holidays. He met Betty and fell in love with her at first sight. Betty and Aidan got married when she was 17 or 18, and she went on to have seven children as well. They had a beautiful house on Highfield Road, and Nana moved in with them. They moved to a house on Rathgar Road then, and Nana came with them and lived there until she died when she was 77. She didn't have bad health, she enjoyed her glass of Powers whiskey in the evening. She had no terrible health issues, she was just quite a frail lady. We don't think of 77 as being old now, but in those days it was. I have lovely memories of my nana who, when you think of it, had an amazing life in the midst of very turbulent times.'

12
Walter Macken

AN EVICTION, AN INDUSTRIAL SCHOOL AND A GREAT WRITER

'He joined a regiment called the Royal Fusiliers in July 1915 and came home and told Agnes he had enlisted. He had no choice really, there was no work and he was the father of three children. So he joined the British army for economic reasons really.'

This story begins in the middle of the nineteenth century when the first Walter Macken was born. His wife was called Mary and they were parents to eleven children, six girls and five boys. He was the chief forester at Ashford Castle, which came with a house. I'm talking to his great-grandson, Ultan Macken, who tells me how disaster hit the family after his great-grandfather died of a heart attack when he was only about 60 years old.

'The landlord, whoever owned Ashford Castle at the time, evicted the family from the house. So they were begging on the side of the road and the boys were arrested and four of them sent to St Joseph's industrial school in Letterfrack, County Galway. I'm almost sure that the girls were also sent off to an orphanage in Galway. The records show that four boys went to Letterfrack; I'm not sure where the fifth boy went. So then Mary Macken, my great-grandmother, moved to Galway and lived on Eyre Street.

'My grandfather, who was called Walter after his father, born in 1882, was in Letterfrack until he was 14 years old. He trained as a carpenter and came to work in Galway. He began working with a group called Emerson Builders, who were a very well-known building company in Galway. He was also a talented actor and singer, and he appeared in a series of melodramas in a place called Racket Court. So he was a carpenter by day and an actor by night.

'Attached to this Racket Court place was a pub, and it was in this pub that he met Agnes Brady, from

Ballinasloe. She was the youngest of 15 children, all of whom had emigrated to America, mainly to Boston. Agnes had one brother, Frank. She was 26 and my grandfather Walter was 20, and he fell in love with her almost immediately. She was very hesitant about marrying him because he was six years younger! There was a very good comedian, Pascal Spellman, whose mother Mrs Spellman worked in the Great Southern Hotel, and she advised my great-grandmother, Mary Macken, that Walter Macken was suitable. They married and their first child Eileen was born in 1911, then Noreen in 1912, and my father, the third Walter, was born in 1915.

'Because of the First World War, there was a kind of a recession in building in Galway, and Emersons told my grandfather that there was no more work for him. He was kind of an impulsive man, and he went to Renmore where there was a huge recruiting campaign going on for men to join the British army. He joined a regiment called the Royal Fusiliers in July 1915 and came home and told Agnes he had enlisted. He had no choice really; there was no work and he was the father of three children. So he joined the British army for economic reasons really.'

Walter Macken was sent to Dover, where he was trained from July to October. 'He wrote a series of letters to my grandmother. My father told me that he remembers seeing my grandfather in a British army uniform, but my mother said that couldn't have been possible as my father was only a baby at the time. But I tracked through my grandfather's letters, and in one of them he says, "I got home, and it was lovely to see you and little Wally in your arms." So my father was correct in remembering that!

'My grandfather was sent to the trenches in December 1915, just before Christmas. Some of his letters give accounts of his time in the trenches, how cold it was and how much snow there was. He kept writing letters to Agnes, every couple of weeks, and there are references to his mother living in Eyre Street with one of his sisters.

> My grandfather was sent to the trenches
> in December 1915, just before Christmas.
> Some of his letters give accounts of his
> time in the trenches, how cold it was
> and how much snow there was.

'Coming towards the Easter Rising time, my grandmother was still working in Racket Court. It was the morning of March 28th and she heard a sound. She looked behind her and there was her husband in full uniform, standing there, and she said, "Wally, you never told me you were coming home!" But it was a vision she saw, it wasn't real. So she knew then that he was dead, and about four days later she got a letter from the chaplain to say that her husband was missing, presumed dead.

'My grandmother then had to try and cope, and raise three children on a British army pension. It was a real love match, what she had with my grandfather, so she was broken-hearted. She insisted on my father sleeping in the bedroom with her, for about six months after that. She used to lay out corpses as part of her work, and she would bring my father with her, which was very traumatic for him.

'My grandmother brought in lodgers to keep things going. There was a lodger upstairs, and the Black and Tans used to drive down the street, but the houses that had someone in the British army in them had been identified with a white mark to denote that they didn't need to be searched. They had that mark on their door, but one night the Black and Tans still beat the hell out of it. My grandmother was terrified, but the lodger ran down the stairs and read the Black and Tans the riot act – "What do you mean by banging on this door, this woman is a widow of the British army" – so they headed off. But in actual fact, the lodger himself was an IRA man with seven rifles upstairs!

The Black and Tans used to drive
down the street, but the houses
that had someone in the British army
in them had been identified with
a white mark to denote that
they didn't need to be searched.

'During my father's growing-up years, his mother used to bring him to mass every morning at 6.30 a.m.; he had this built into him, this devotion. So at the age of 12 or 13 he decided he wanted to become a priest. He consulted his mother and she recommended he talk to the Jesuits about this. He had been to primary school in the Presentation convent. He spent two years there and his sisters were there too. He was intrigued by the little inkwell where you dipped your pen, and about a week after starting in the school he drank the ink! The poor nun was horrified – she called his sister Noreen to come down and wash his face. In later years he wrote a piece for the Presentation centenary yearbook about it; he said that ever since he drank the ink, it took him all these years to get rid of it, by writing it out of himself.

'Every summer my father and his sisters would be sent to Ballinasloe to work on the family farm with my grandmother's brother. It was less expense on my grandmother, to have them out of the house. My father was set to work weeding a ten-acre fields of turnips. All that time in Ballinasloe was material for his novel *The Bogman*. He was so aware of what was going on in the village he lived in.

'His mother and the children moved from one council house on St Joseph's Avenue, when he was 12, to a bigger one on Henry Street, around the corner. They had two lodgers. My father hated that, that they had strangers in the house with him. Afterwards, we never had anyone stay in our house because of that. My father went from the Presentation convent school to The Bish, which was the Patrician Brothers secondary school. He was delighted to make the move. He made his confirmation in Presentation before he left.

'He told me again and again how the Black and Tans in their lorry would drive up and down the street, terrifying them. They were also scared of the police, the RIC. They carried pistols and when the lads would be playing games on the corner, two RIC men would chase the boys and frighten them with their pistols.

'My father used to get into a lot of fights on the street and Noreen would rescue him from them. I asked him once, "Did you like school?" He didn't! I don't think it was challenging enough for him, the way it was taught. And there was a lot of corporal punishment too, not so much for him, but he witnessed it. He wrote an autobiographical book, which I haven't published yet, with some awful descriptions of the punishment meted out.

'My father, the way he used to write … he had this system. He went to mass every morning at eight o'clock, bought *The Irish Press*, came home, had his breakfast and then went into the living room and worked on whatever piece he was writing at the time, play or short story or novel. He would then read it directly to my mother. They were very, very close. My father really cared what my mother thought of his writing; she influenced his writing in that way. That's why when my father died suddenly at the age of 51, on 22 April 1967, I decided to give up my work in *The Sunday Press* and come back to live with her for a couple of years.'

He went to mass every morning at eight o'clock, bought The Irish Press, came home, had his breakfast and then went into the living room and worked on whatever piece he was writing at the time, play or short story or novel. He would then read it directly to my mother.

Ultan, who was born in 1943 when his father was director of the Taibhdhearc theatre in Galway, has worked as a writer, a broadcaster, a journalist and an actor (he has a one-man show called *My Father, My Son*). He has published a number of books, including a biography of his father, *Dreams on Paper*.

As part of his freelance radio work, Ultan used to interview people in pop music. 'In 1977 I heard that Bing Crosby was staying in the Gresham hotel, so I went to the Gresham and asked if I could talk to him. He kept me waiting for six hours, in the lounge. Eventually I got up to do the interview. One of the things I was most interested in was how he came to record "Galway Bay". He almost dismissed it; he said

Walter Macken and his sons, Ultan and Wally.

he walked into the studio and the producer said, "Here's a song for you," so he sang it! Afterwards I went in to Billy Wall, a producer in RTÉ radio, and said, "I have this interview with Bing Crosby" – but I hadn't been sent there officially so he wasn't interested in it. About three months later, Bing Crosby died! So Billy Wall rang me at 7 a.m. and said, "Have you got that tape?" But they edited out my voice completely! I passed by Val Joyce in RTÉ later on that day and he said, "Oh, I liked your interview with Bing Crosby." And I asked how he knew it was me. There was one question I had asked Bing that was so close they couldn't edit it out. So he recognised my voice.'

In 1977 I heard that Bing Crosby was staying in the Gresham hotel, so I went to the Gresham and asked if I could talk to him. He kept me waiting for six hours.

Ultan remembers the family's early years when they lived on Grattan Road near the strand that leads out to Salthill. 'My father was working in the Taibhdhearc. My first four years of life, I have no memory of him. My mother and brother were the centre of my life. My father did 77 original plays and productions in the nine years he was in the Taibhdhearc. He moved to the Abbey then and looked around Dublin to find a place for us all to stay. When he found somewhere he got my mother to bring us up on the train. That's my first memory of him. It was the Galway train, a steam engine with smoke and windows that you could put up and down, and I remember coming into Westland Row and looking out the window. I could see my father running towards us. We got a taxi, and he brought us to the flat he had rented temporarily beside the canal, behind Croke Park.

'My mother spent days and weeks walking the roads and eventually found us a house in Cabra, near Phoenix Park. That's where we lived for the few years when Dad worked in the Abbey. Then he got the leading part in a play called *The King of Friday's Men* by M.J. Molloy, which opened in October 1948. It was hugely successful, and an American theatre producer came to see it. His name was Mike Grace. He asked my father to come to America with the play. At the time, only one actor from abroad was allowed go with a play to America. My father went and did a six-month tour; my mother accompanied him, and my grandmother came to stay with us. She was the storyteller: she is the origins of the storytelling that both my father and myself have in us. She talked to me all the time and I listened to her.'

While Walter Macken was on Broadway, his novel *Rain on the Wind* was published and was chosen as the Book of the Month Club choice for the Literary Guild awards. That meant guaranteed sales of half a million copies and meant that he could afford to become a full-time writer. 'With the success of the book, he came back to Dublin; he resigned from the Abbey and went to Galway to look for a house. My mother didn't go with him, which was unusual. He drove out to Oughterard and he found this house. The house was three thousand pounds, and he sent a telegram to his publishers, Macmillan, to tell them that he had found a house and how much it was, and they wired him back the money straight away!

'The funny part of it was he came back to Dublin all excited, he had bought the house and everything, and my mother started to quiz him about it. He told her about the rhododendrons and the azaleas and the cherry tree, and about the tennis court and the orchard, and she said, "Walter, what about the house?" And he hadn't gone into the house at all! He didn't go in the door! He was just so bowled over by the setting and the garden. It had a boathouse and a boat with it. He loved fishing. I loved the house too; it's out of the family now, though. Nearly all of his books were written while he was there. He rarely went away after that; he got into his routine of writing there.

He told her about the rhododendrons
and the azaleas and the cherry tree, and
about the tennis court and the orchard,
and she said, 'Walter, what about the
house?' And he hadn't gone into
the house at all! He didn't go in the
door! He was just so bowled over
by the setting and the garden.

'When Walter went to America he met his aunts,
his father's sisters. They had moved to New York and
worked as house cleaners, and they had married the
owners of the houses and become wealthy women!
He was very taken by them, but he was shocked by
their outlook on Ireland.

'They viewed it as a terrible place that no one
would want to live in. My grandfather's brothers,
John and Tom, who lived in England, and Michael
who lived in Canada, had all volunteered for the
British army. Tom and John survived, and John came
to visit us in the 1950s. John had a pronounced
north of England accent, which put my father off
straight away, but on top of that, he had divorced his
first wife and married a second lady.

'We had a test for people, my father and I. We
would bring them out on the boat on Lough Corrib
for the day, show them the mountains and the islands

and the beauty of it all. It was kind of a test run with everybody. We brought uncle John out anyway, and showed him the monastery on Inchagoill, and my father said, "Well, John, what do you think of this?" And John said, "Well, I don't think much of it, actually." It's only now that I realise we were actually right opposite where he had grown up with his family, from where he had been evicted and sent to Letterfrack, so why would he be happy to be there?

'I read everything my father wrote, and I remember being so intrigued by where he got all his information. I remember him saying, "Ultan, in a hundred years' time, when people sit down to read my stories, they will say 'That is how people lived.'"

What he did, with people, he would listen to them, and get them to tell him their life stories. He was absorbing it all and incorporating it into his writing.

Walter and his wife, Peggy.

'When I read the books now, I can see the origin material. When he was writing *Rain on the Wind*, at that time in Ireland every family would have ten children in it; it would never be just two brothers. It was a reflection on us, our family. The young son wanted to go on fishing trips with the father, and the older son was the mother's favourite, which was exactly our family situation. My brother always did what he was told, and I was always in trouble. I questioned everybody. I had an English teacher, one year we were doing *Hamlet*. My father got me to read a book all about *Hamlet*, so I knew more than the poor teacher, and I was questioning him!

'I remember when my dad died. What happened was that I came home for Easter in 1967. We were living in Menlo then. It was my mother's idea to move out of the house in Oughterard. I don't think my father wanted to move at all. He was upset about that. He chose this lovely village, Menlo. He built the house out of the proceeds of one of his books. It was a perfect little village at the time; there were only 300 locals living there. I came home at Easter, I was working for *The Sunday Press*. I used to go out for these big long walks with him, on the prom, all the way out to Silver Strand and back again. We would talk about everything and anything. This was about four weeks before he died. My mother was very depressed and I mentioned it to my father.

I asked why she was depressed. He said, "You don't worry about your mother, I'll look after her." But I think my mother, instinctively, was anticipating what was going to happen. I just have a feeling about it.

'The last week of his life, he was sent to Calvary hospital by his doctor, to do a series of tests.

'He had stomach upsets, they thought it might be a hernia. He was a week in hospital, working away on whatever project he was doing, got on great with all the nurses and doctors and everybody. On the Friday, he was released from hospital at about four o'clock. He and my mother went for a walk on the prom; they came back for their tea, he had his usual fry-up. In the evening they watched television, and at eleven o'clock they went to bed as normal. He couldn't sleep that night, and he said to my mother that he would go out and lie on the sofa, which he often used to do in the afternoon.

'Meanwhile, I was in Dublin; he had rung me that afternoon to tell me he had been discharged from hospital and they thought he might need a minor operation on a hernia or something. At the time, I used to sing in a folk club on Harcourt Street, which usually ran from 10 p.m. to 4 a.m., but that particular night I came home at 2 a.m., and I couldn't sleep. At 5 a.m. I got a call from my brother's organisation, Opus Dei, to say that my father was very seriously ill and that my brother and I had to drive to Galway immediately. I got ready, and Wally, my brother, came along. My father had given me his old car, which didn't have a radio in it, but my brother brought his car, and it had a radio. So we drove in his car, and at 8 a.m. I wanted to hear the news, so we turned on the radio and the third item was "Walter Macken died at his home in Menlo this morning". So that is how we heard of our father's death. What had happened was that my mother's step-brother, Ivor Kenny, used to be a newsreader for Raidió Éireann, so once he heard of the death, he realised its importance and contacted the newsroom. He assumed that Opus Dei would tell us that my father was dead, but they didn't. They were being kind, I suppose, but it was a hard way to hear it.

'We drove to Galway anyway, to Calvary hospital, and my uncle Mick stopped us at the gateway and brought us into the morgue, and we prayed with my father's body for half an hour. We went from there to Mick's house; he was married to my mother's sister May. May had gone and collected my mother. We walked in the door, and my mother just embraced the two of us. She had this look of joy when she saw us, and I never saw that look again in the 25 years she lived after. She was happy to see us in that minute, but she mourned her husband so badly.

> We walked in the door, and my mother
> just embraced the two of us. She had this
> look of joy when she saw us, and
> I never saw that look again in the
> 25 years she lived after. She was happy
> to see us in that minute, but
> she mourned her husband so badly.

'My mother, Peggy Kenny, had made such a sacrifice. She was a professional journalist when she met my father, and my father was simply an actor. She was working in the *Connacht Tribune*; her father, Tom "Cork" Kenny, had founded the paper in 1909, the year my mother was born.

'I stayed at home for three years after my father died. I established a routine for my mother every day. I drove her to mass, and I did her shopping with her, and I was writing a lot as well. Eventually I got jobs as a teacher and a few other things. During those three years, I met my future wife, Mary Burns from Ballycroy, in Galway university. I wouldn't have met her otherwise. She was only 19 when I met her in 1969. The moon landing was going on until 2 a.m., and we were in Menlo watching it. So that was the amazing thing, really, meeting her. Three weeks after I met her, my mother said, "You're going to marry that girl!" I don't know how she knew that!

'I am very, very proud of my father, and I am blessed to have had parents like I had. Both of them were deprived of love when they were young, so they set out to give unconditional love to myself and my brother. I was fortunate to meet Mary, with whom I had this wonderful romance and love, even though it broke up eventually, but we had 20 years together and three children. We kept in contact, despite the fact that we were separated. She eventually married and divorced another fellow, but we stayed in contact up until she died, in 2013, at the age of 64. She got non-Hodgkin's lymphoma back in 2005, and she was eight years battling cancer. We kept a great, deep friendship all our lives, and never lost it.'

Ultan has three daughters, Caoimhe, Roisin and Áine. 'Caoimhe, my eldest girl, arranged for me to go and see Mary three Sundays before she died. The three girls were there, and we talked really openly, and I apologised for any hurt I ever caused her, and she apologised to me, and it was like we were back together again, almost.

'The following Sunday was the last time I saw her, and she said, "Ultan, I'm worried, I don't know where I'm going." And I said, "You're after suffering eight years of cancer, you're going straight to Heaven, I'm sure of it." I think my family has a way of seeing forces outside of ourselves, like the way my grandmother witnessed my grandfather. In the same way, after my father died, about three months later, I came home and I had this dream, and in the dream I could see my father. My daughters had the same experience.

The following Sunday was the last time I
saw her, and she said, 'Ultan, I'm worried,
I don't know where I'm going.' And I said,
'You're after suffering eight years of
cancer, you're going straight to Heaven,
I'm sure of it.'

'When I was about 12, I decided to become a writer. I began writing a novel called *The Thrashing Floor*. I don't think it was because of my father, but one great thing I had was that I wrote short stories and my father read them before he died, and he liked them.'

13
William Ross

A REVOLVER UNDER THE PILLOW

'We're always looking backwards and making judgements, but in the type of world that people inhabited then there was a lot of neighbourliness. For every atrocity, there was something good.'

On 7 June 1917, Major Willie Redmond, MP for East Clare, was killed in action in the First World War at Messines in Belgium. The by-election that followed introduced the young Éamon de Valera to the national stage. De Valera lodged his nomination papers for the by-election in the old military barracks in Ennis under the supervision of the RIC sergeant, William Ross.

I am chatting with William's grandson, Mervyn Taylor. 'My grandfather was born in the townland of Rowry, near Rosscarbery in west Cork in 1879. As a young man he was thinking of emigrating but joined the RIC instead. He was a Freemason, but he was not an Orangeman. The Freemasons were a benevolent fund, a men's club, but very much for mutual help. We're always looking backwards and making judgements, but in the type of world that people inhabited then there was a lot of neighbourliness. For every atrocity, there was something good.

'I was researching back to the time when my grandfather was in Ennis, and I read through some of the military archives of the IRA in Clare, and there were some wonderful things in there as well as the shootings. In one instance they were to attack an RIC barracks but they knew the sergeant's wife wasn't well, so they didn't really go too hard on the barracks!

In one instance they were to attack
an RIC barracks but they knew the
sergeant's wife wasn't well, so they didn't
really go too hard on the barracks!

'There were extraordinarily brutal things done too, though. My grandfather's view was the

William and Maria Ross.

standard view, that the Black and Tans were the scum of the English prisons. But they weren't. The Auxiliaries, as opposed to the Black and Tans, some of them were very brave. It wasn't just the Black and Tans, some of the other regiments too were quite undisciplined, and that's why my grandfather would have put the door on the latch and some food out, so that they mightn't think of looking in the RIC man's house for weapons. Some of the 'Tans were regular army men, who had been through war. The Auxiliaries on the other hand were British military drafted in to assist the RIC against the IRA.

'My grandfather left school very young. He worked around the farm, but the land around Rowry wasn't great. Nothing but rock and gorse, a few good fields. Ireland was a rural country and he grew up on the land, and when they were back in Wicklow they would have had some land. My father would have always been a small farmer too. My cousin Matt spoke of him as being a very, very tough man, very hard-working.'

William married a girl called Maria Patterson from Conna, County Cork on 9 December 1909 and the couple went on to have three children: Annie (Mervyn's mother), John and Maura. As an RIC man William was involved with signals and codes and communications. 'He was stationed in Nenagh during the War of Independence and Civil War. They were close neighbours and friends of the Bergin family in Silver Street. My mother always spoke very fondly of the Bergins, one of whose daughters used to come and stay with her every so often. When my grandfather died in 1958, the funeral was in County Wicklow. The Bergins were very put out because they had travelled up to attend but had gone to the wrong "gap", the Wicklow Gap instead of the Sally Gap.

'My grandfather slept with a revolver under his pillow – he had to. During the Civil War, my mother remembered the wails of the widows of RIC men who'd been killed, but she also remembered the next-door neighbours. During the fighting periods – Tipperary was quite anti-treaty – the lady next door in Nenagh put her head out the door and got the tip of her nose taken off by a gunshot. A lot of people had joined the IRA and it was pretty bitter, and for safety reasons my grandfather decided to get out. The RIC had been disbanded, and so they left Ireland and went to live in a little English village called Almeley in Herefordshire. It was absolutely lawless at that point. There were 126 people killed in County Tipperary during the Civil War.

My grandfather slept with a revolver
under his pillow – he had to. During
the Civil War, my mother remembered
the wails of the widows of RIC
men who'd been killed.

'In 1930, my grandparents came back to Ireland, to Knockraheen near Roundwood in County Wicklow, where they worked a small farm. They kept in touch with the Bergins, and one day Mick Bergin said to my grandfather, "You needn't have gone away, you know, you wouldn't have been touched." But he knew he had to go, for his own safety and that of his family.

'When I was a child in Roundwood there were people my mother would always visit, including the Hattons, who lived in a townland past the reservoir and over the hill. The Hattons were very friendly and had a great welcome for my mother. The grandfather was very much a de Valera man, and my grandfather used to say that the problem with Ireland was that the working people didn't vote for their party.

'My aunt Maura got married and she was living down in Limerick. My uncle John emigrated when we were kids. My grandfather was not an imperialist; he was good friends with Mick Bergin and that friendship lasted. My mother got married late; it was common in those days. Her family were extremely industrious people, with amazing skills. They made their own black pudding and butter, and my mother had a cert that showed she got 98 per cent for her butter-making! She was a very practical woman. She taught me how to skin a rabbit for eating, would you believe – now that was a skill to have, skinning an animal! People in those days had a lot of farmyard skills and survival skills. One of my mother's greatest put-downs would be if someone came to the house and brought a cake, she'd say, "Oh well, that was a *bought* cake." Not so much an insult but a very strict judgement; in other words, they weren't able to look after themselves and make a cake!

One of my mother's greatest put-downs
would be if someone came to the house
and brought a cake, she'd say, 'Oh well,
that was a bought cake.'

'When my mother met my father they were both living in County Wicklow. There were two churches you could go to: one was Calary – both of my parents are buried there – and the other Derralossary, where my grandparents are buried. My parents got married in 1945. My father would have been in Ballinastoe, and when they got married they lived in Liscolman on the Carlow/Wicklow border. Then my brother and sister were born, and before I was born my father developed a tremor in his leg which was later diagnosed as MS. He got a job as a steward on the Tynte estate in Dunlavin; it couldn't have been too many years he was there, and he was in hospital when I was born in 1958.

'Old Miss Tynte was one of the founders of the Royal Irish Automobile Club. We lived in the upper lodge and when my father got sick we went to live in the lower lodge, two separate houses on the estate. The dying out of that estate is really the end of an era, the fin de siècle. Most of those landowners were dying out at that period, apart from the ones who were burnt out. It was an age of remarkable change in one way. These were the years of independence and moving from Protestant to Catholic. I grew up as a Protestant, and there were very different conventions.

Most of those landowners were dying
out at that period, apart from the ones
who were burnt out. It was an age of
remarkable change in one way.

'My memories are very much based on my
mother's stories. I remember she used to tune in to
The Archers. We had a very rich cultural background
because my mother was a good singer and a church
organist. The village in England where she grew up
was near the Welsh border and she had a Welsh music
teacher. She had a great appreciation of Welsh and
English folk music, as well as Clare folk music. She
listened to a lot of *céilí* music, but my father wasn't
into that: he was a GAA man. My mother had a great
appreciation of both cultures, and that's why it was
interesting that Sheila Bergin, the daughter, came to
the house to stay and Mum would try to talk to her
about politics, but she was a very apolitical woman
even though one of her brothers was killed in the
closing days of the War of Independence.

'My grandfather lived until 1958. He had a small
RIC pension. He had a certain amount of bitterness in
later life; he had been taking on extra responsibilities
as a sergeant, but that hadn't been recognised when
he was de-mobbed, and he felt that he was sold down
the Swanee by his former employer, Her Majesty.

'My grandmother was quite a stern character, and my grandfather would just go along with her, I think. Men made big decisions, but a huge amount of the power was vested in the women at the time. They had a lot of power in the home.

> Men made big decisions, but a huge amount of the power was vested in the women at the time. They had a lot of power in the home.

'Ms Tynte was a classic character; she was unmarried, and both respected and feared. She was very much of another class. I'm one of those people who can genuinely remember a landlord. She would come into the house and everybody's back would straighten. She was decent enough to my father – she gave him the lower lodge to live in when he couldn't work. He tried to run things from a pony and trap, but he ended up falling one day and had to drag himself home a few miles on his hands and knees. It became increasingly hard for him to work due to the MS, and because my mother was older and couldn't manage the house, we moved to a cottage in Annamoe when I was six. Some of the Tynte family didn't have any children, and before we moved they approached my father and said, "Times are hard for you and you have another mouth to feed. Why don't we take your son off your hands and rear him for you?" It would have been common enough then, but not across classes like that. Maybe within families. My daughter still asks me why they didn't do that – she could have been Lady Tynte!

'In Tynte Park there was a crossroads, and our nearest neighbours were the Englishes. We got the water from a pump which was halfway down to the next farm, or from a big well, and we carried it back to the house; we had no electricity or running water in those days. It was incredibly quiet, but in the summer the Irish army would be out on training exercises and you would hear artillery fire. Their vehicles were forever breaking down and they would be up looking for water, for the radiators. Then there was the Kildare hunt that came on Stephen's Day, and when you're a kid and seeing the top hats and the fancy outfits and the ladies riding side-saddle, horses and riders getting separated, dogs getting lost during the hunt … there was plenty of excitement for a small child.

> We got the water from a pump which was halfway down to the next farm, or from a big well, and we carried it back to the house; we had no electricity or running water in those days.

'I started school when I was in Tynte Park. I walked from Tynte Park to Dunlavin national school; it was three miles. By the time I was finishing school there was a van that brought us. Our house, the lower lodge, had a chapel, where there were services held every so often. There was a door that led from our bedroom directly into the chapel, to where the pews were. When you're a kid, all of these things have greater scale. But it was still unusual having a little church attached to your house. There were three of us: the eldest was my brother Hubert, then my sister Noeleen, and myself. And we're all still alive. I was so good at getting married, I did it twice – first in 1979, and again in 2006.

'Why I'm called Mervyn could have something to do with a Major Mervyn Tynte, who died in Burma when fighting in the First World War. It would have been a way of recognising the family's loss.

'Ms Tynte would have been living in a foreign state back then really, being a product of the old imperial world. There would have been no question of her being friends with us; my father was trusted because he was the steward, but that's it.

'We sometimes minded the big house when they were away. I have vague memories of being in there. They had a telephone, and believe me, nothing on the internet beats watching someone going over to the wall, winding this thing up, getting through to the operator in Dunlavin and saying, "What's the time? … Thanks very much." Just to see if you could actually talk to somebody in the next town! It was an amazing piece of technology. That and the radio had a far greater impact than anything we have now. We look back and see how primitive the technology was, but then you think, historically, how incredible it was.

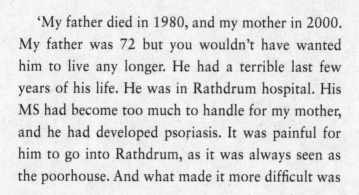

> They had a telephone, and believe
> me, nothing on the internet
> beats watching someone going
> over to the wall, winding this thing up,
> getting through to the operator
> in Dunlavin and saying, "What's the
> time? … Thanks very much."

'My father died in 1980, and my mother in 2000. My father was 72 but you wouldn't have wanted him to live any longer. He had a terrible last few years of his life. He was in Rathdrum hospital. His MS had become too much to handle for my mother, and he had developed psoriasis. It was painful for him to go into Rathdrum, as it was always seen as the poorhouse. And what made it more difficult was that he was brought up as a devout Prod, and in Rathdrum he was medicated and under a Sacred Heart, one of these electrical things that come out of the wall and light up. He wanted to be at home, but the services weren't there. It was so rough, and sort of a release when the end came. My mother got another 20 years; she was 87 when she died.'

14
Mary Langan

THE BIGGEST REBEL
OF THEM ALL

'I remember my father in the coffin.
I was staying with my aunt Freda
and my grandmother made me
come down and see him and say
goodbye to him. It was dreadful.'

'They lived in a funny kind of farmhouse. At one side of the fireplace was a press, but when you opened it, there was a stairs that went up to a bedroom over the parlour. As you came in the kitchen door, there was a dresser at the end wall, and there was a little triangle taken out of it and that meant there was another stairs leading up to another bedroom that happened to be underneath. They were for people who were on the run. They would come and stay a night, have a bite to eat and be on the run again.'

This was the childhood home of 87-year-old Maureen Doyle in the parish of Kilmaine in County Mayo. 'We are the last parish on the southern point of the county and it was so remote, this village, that I don't think the roads were even fit to take the Black and Tans. They would have been on the main road to Galway, but not this little place. It was a good place to hide.'

But even though it was the perfect hiding place, the Civil War had divided families and communities. 'Some people were sympathetic to the rebels and some were not. There was a divide, even within families. The Civil War was a terrible time, brothers shot brothers, a very, very tough time.'

> Some people were sympathetic to the rebels and some were not. There was a divide, even within families. The Civil War was a terrible time, brothers shot brothers, a very, very tough time.

Maureen is remembering her maternal grandmother, Mary Langan, 'the biggest rebel of them all. A real republican. She would shelter people who were fighting, even though they only had this small farmhouse at the back of the parish. The family had a pub in the village of Shrule. It was called The Highway Inn, and it is still there, but it's not the family running the business anymore. It was the halfway house between Galway and Castlebar, and these men used to drive with two horses and deliver

Mary Langan.

the groceries from the wholesale grocers in towns like Ballinrobe and Westport, and they stayed overnight in Shrule. So they had somebody to look after the horses in the yard, and in the morning they got breakfast and continued the journey. You wouldn't make it from Galway to Castlebar in one day in those days. Especially in the wintertime, when the evenings were so short.

'I don't know how my grandmother found somebody to marry in the middle of nowhere but she did! She was just brilliant. She delivered the babies and loved where she lived, in a place called the Valley of the Flies, Cluainameeltogue, the Anglicisation of the Irish words.

'It was a very remote village, and the anti-treaty rebels could hide there and take a rest for a day or two, before going on and doing whatever it was they had to do. I know the RIC barracks in Shrule was burned down.'

The barracks had in fact been closed but was about to reopen when it was burned. Two of the rebels involved in the operation were injured when explosives inside the building, which some believe had been put under the stairs by the RIC, detonated. Those who carried out the arson attack were looked after in the local safe houses, but one of the two men caught up in the explosion, John Joe Keleghan, was badly burned and died a couple of weeks later.

Mary Langan was only 19 when she married Laurence O'Dea, and they went on to have eight children, four boys and four girls. 'One little girl died of pneumonia when she was six years old; they couldn't cure it in those days.

'I don't think Laurence was a republican, to be honest. He didn't take part in too much; he was not a very strong man. He had fallen off a horse at one time and there was one rib pressing on a muscle in his heart, and when that would happen and he would faint when out ploughing the fields, he'd have to go home and rest for a few days. He wasn't a very healthy man but he lived to be 91!

'I remember when we used to go to visit my grandparents. Myself and my first cousin Mary, my aunt Freda's daughter, used to go every Friday after school, walking the three or four miles in our bare feet to go up to Shrule and collect their pensions for them. Of my grandparents' eight children, the first-born, Willie, was the only one to emigrate to America. I think there must have been an accident because he was only there a short while and they got word he had died. Then there was Martin, and Patrick, and Richard – we always called him uncle Dick. They all settled at home, all of them were farmers. Uncle Dick's wife Esther came from Shrule as well; she only died two years ago, and she was 99. She died the 8th of December and she would have been 100 in March – they thought she would make the 100. My mother was Mary Kate – she was the eldest of the girls. Then there was Freda, Anne (she was the little one who died) and then Nora.

'I have a feeling that a lot of the rebels involved in the Civil War made a pact afterwards that they would not discuss what happened. No matter what you asked them, you would not get an explanation.

'Nora married a man called Paddy Macken, and my mother was married to a John Macken – they weren't related, they came from different villages too. Freda married an RIC man, Canny. He probably would have had a lot of information, but he didn't give any of it away. They're all a long time dead, those men.

'I go back to the area very often; my own brother is still there. I had two brothers and they would smoke anything at all. Woodbine and everything. They all smoked back then; they'd all sit around the fire and smoke cigarettes, and you'd have to leave the kitchen because they'd smoke you out of it, my eyes would be hurting! My grandmother lived and died in the same house; she was about 83 when she died.

'My mother went to a place in the north of Ireland called Aughnacloy to train as a milliner. There was a hat factory in Ballinrobe, you see, and every man

back then wore a felt hat. You had to do this training course to be a milliner, and she always said that she made my uncle Dick's first communion suit.

Davey Macken, Maureen Doyle's uncle from Mayo, who emigrated to New Zealand.

She was 21 years older than Dick and was so proud that she was able to make his suit for him. She learned so much from that course. At that time there would be a bus bringing people in third-level education to various balls, and you'd see them coming down the road in their long dresses, and she would have to shorten their hems for them or whatever. She would love those jobs.

'We were about two minutes outside the village of Kilmaine, on a farm as well. My mother had a very tough life, but she got on with it. She kept cows, hens, pigs, ducks. I don't know how she did it. She had four children. I'm the eldest and we're all still alive. My brother Davey is still on the farm and working away. He foots turf all day; he is 6 foot 2 but he has kneelers and pads for his knees and all. He is 86, a year younger than me. My sister Siobhán lives in Dublin and my younger brother Frank is living in England, in Reading.

'I remember the day my father died. I was only ten years old. I was in the church waiting in a queue to go for confession. The church was just outside the village of Kilmaine. Next thing the priest was called out of the confessional and headed off, and the older priest went in. Later, I was on my way home and I met the priest, and he got off his bike and he said, "You look like one of the Mackens" – we all had white hair and looked very alike. We used to be called the Herefords because of our hair! Anyway, I said, "Yes, I am." And he said, "I'm afraid I have to tell you your father just died." I had a bag of groceries in my hand; I ran home as fast as I could, threw the bag in the door. At that stage the house was full of people and I ran up to my aunt Freda in the village.

'I remember my father in the coffin. I was staying with my aunt Freda and my grandmother made me come down and see him and say goodbye to him. It was dreadful. He was in the bedroom; everything was gone out of the room, it was only the coffin. That was my first experience of death. I remember being in the graveyard afterwards with my aunt. That was it, he was gone. It was very sad.

'My uncles were close at hand afterwards. We had great neighbours, and they helped us with the farm. I was eventually sent to boarding school in Claremorris. It was fine, I didn't hate it. At least we didn't have to weed the turnips there!

'My grandmother was a great woman, a really wonderful woman. She used to take us and sit us on the wall in front of her house and point up to the hills in Connemara and say, "There's the Twelve Pins now, and some days they are all visible" – and she'd make us count them together. And the aurora borealis or northern lights, she would teach us about it and take us out to look for it. I could have killed her in those days. I didn't want to be counting the Twelve Pins – but wasn't she great to know all about that and to teach us about them!

> And the aurora borealis or northern
> lights, she would teach us about it
> and take us out to look for it.

'I don't ever remember her or my grandfather going to mass, but they lived so far away from the church: it was a long, long walk across the fields. I'm sure they went when they were younger, but when they got older it was very difficult. That's why we had to get their pensions for them on a Friday. We'd spend the whole weekend with them and be sent off to mass on a Sunday and then home again.

'When I left school, I answered an ad in the paper for a junior teaching assistant in Redcross in County Wicklow. It was a case of taking the job I was offered or going back to school, and I thought to myself, sure it would be one of us off Mammy's back. The parish priest collected me off the train; his name was Fr Mulcahy. I went to live in Redcross, in a lovely old vicarage house in the centre of the village. There were three of us teachers there. One of them, Mary Flynn, my best friend of 68 years, died in April, that was an awful shock. We lived together until we got married and she moved to Roscommon. We were very close.

'When I moved to Redcross in 1952 there wasn't very much to do, only buy a bicycle and cycle around the place. The school was only 100 yards up the road from the vicarage. I met my husband Michael in the local hall. I knew him for a few years before we got married in 1959, and we had 13 children: Jimmy, Hilda, John (who we lost five years ago), Martin and Joe who are twins, then Maude, Mary, Eilish, Sinead, Una, Tom, Michael and Hugh. Hugh is the baby, he's 42 now. John was a garda sergeant in Terenure in Dublin. He was only six months into his retirement when he became ill. It was terrible, the worst thing ever.

'You're going to drop when you hear this: I have 40 grandchildren! Three generations of the family are teachers. My children Maude, Jimmy, Mary, Una and Tom are all teachers and my granddaughter Aislinn and grandson Davey are teachers too!

'I tell you what, though, if I didn't have religion I would have given up. Especially when John died, and then my husband Michael died very suddenly as well. Michael had a sister, Valerie, living in Enniscorthy, and before Christmas 14 years ago we decided to go down and see her. We came home that evening, and he had a fine big tea. It was two herrings, herrings from Wicklow, and he said after the news at nine o'clock that he was going to go to bed. Didn't I stay up writing Christmas cards, until about half past eleven, and when I got up to bed, he said, "Do you know what, I have a pain in my chest, and I can't get rid of it."

I tell you what, though, if I didn't have religion I would have given up.

'I hit the pillow and was nearly asleep, when he gave me an elbow about two minutes later and said, "I think we better get the Caredoc." Well, did I hop out of the bed then! I rang Maude and Jimmy – one lives each side of me – and they came. The ambulance arrived, and Michael wasn't that bad really; he got out of the bed in his pyjamas and went to use the bathroom, and when he was coming back Jimmy was standing at the bed and he said, "Watch out, Dad, you look like you're about to fall", and he put out his arms to him, and Michael was gone by the time he caught him. It was so sad. Fourteen years ago now. The kids were grown up or in college at that point. Michael was taken up to Loughlinstown to the morgue, and we all went up and spent the night with him there, and he came home in the morning. That was it. That was the 13th of December 2007.'

15
Martin Curley

DELIGHT AT
THE NEW SPUDS

'As a kid, I remember in early
December, getting these magical
Christmas cards from America.
Something about the American
stamps, with the address on a
label, the luxury of the envelope,
it was magical!'

This story begins in the small village of Guilka near Menlough in east Galway. Local historian Martin Curley is a hive of information about his family and the life of the village and beyond against the unrest of the 1920s.

'My grandfather, Patrick Curley, at the time of the troubles back in 1916 was a man of 40 years of age. He was married two years at that point to Kate Gormley. They started their family: my aunt Julia was born in 1915 and my father Martin was born in 1917. Patrick and Kate went on to have eight children. Just down the road from their home was a place called Springlawn. The Irish Republican Brotherhood (IRB), or the Fenians, to give it its American name, were quite active there. I live in Mountbellew, and in 1833 Colonel Thomas Kelly, who became the leader of the IRB, was born here. The IRB has deep roots and goes back 200 years to the Whiteboys, the Ribbonmen, and there was a monument to a man named Ned Lohan not too far from where I grew up. He was executed in 1820 for the attempted assassination of one of the landlords. The landlord that they were meant to assassinate was not the landlord that they actually tried to assassinate.

'Another notable local was James Haverty, who left for England 120 years ago and worked in Blackpool for a while. He came back and started an egg business, as in going around and buying eggs from farmers. He was doing well for himself, but was also very much a nationalist. He wrote multiple times to the local newspapers about the political events of the day and organised the Springlawn Volunteers in the early 1910s. They even made the front cover of the *London Illustrated News* in 1914. Someone took a picture of them lined up outside

James Haverty's house. There were about three or four guns, that was it, and the local military man giving them drilling orders. In the middle of all this, there were Sinn Féin clubs springing up all over the place. I'll tell you about a relation of mine. His name was Jack Keogh. My grandfather's uncle was Bernard Curley. Bernard had married twice – the first wife was a widow, Widow Scully as she was known. She had no children and died soon afterwards. Then Bernard married Ellen Hansberry, and they had three daughters. Unfortunately, Ellen passed away as well, so the three girls were sent out to live with various aunts and uncles and, in our house, one of the girls, Ellen Jr, was living.

'Two of the girls married local men but Ellen Jr went to America and married Jack Keogh. Jack Keogh was from Ballinasloe originally and emigrated to America. Smuggled in, more than likely, because he had escaped from prison in Dublin around 1925. He fought in the War of Independence and afterwards took the anti-treaty side. He was a scourge for the newly established government, and eventually was arrested. In America he met Ellen Jr, my grandfather's first cousin, and they had a number of children. They came back to Ireland but Jack died in quite tragic circumstances in the 1940s. Beer bottles were found at the scene of his death, but it wasn't beer that was in the bottles. People at the time reused glass bottles, often keeping poison in them. Jack had been accidentally poisoned.

'Jack Keogh would have been one of those guys, whenever anything happened in Ballinasloe from 1922 on, it would have been blamed on him. Even before that, when he was a young lad, his brother, who was only 19, had died in awful circumstances. A number of locals were trying to stop something from happening, stop somebody from getting arrested, and the young lad died. Jack seemed to take it personally against some of the people, and from then on he was held responsible for everything that happened in Ballinasloe or Portumna or anywhere around. He was a central figure in the movement. He would have been very active and would have inspired people to take the anti-treaty side, but he couldn't have been personally responsible for each of the incidents – no. He couldn't get around that fast! Ellen only passed away in 1995, aged 88.

'Guilka had a post office and a pub, back in the day, so it was a hive of activity. In December 1920, the Menlough RIC detained a Joyce man who was going around teaching Irish as part of the Gaelic League and held him without trial or evidence for several days. This drew the ire of the priest in Caltra called Fr Malachy Brennan, who was an amazing character. He wrote plenty of letters criticising the government. At one point he was brought before the court for something or other, and he refused to take off his hat! One of those subtle ways of defiance.

He wrote plenty of letters criticising the government. At one point he was brought before the court for something or other, and he refused to take off his hat! One of those subtle ways of defiance.

'Around the same time, there was a large gathering of young men in Menlough Hall, and the RIC came and started snooping, and one of them said he overheard a criticism of the amount of money that was being paid by Ireland to Britain. So they went in and took names and asked them what they were doing – they said they were getting trees for forestry. So they were brought up on trial, and one of them refused to acknowledge the court.

'The sergeant gave his account of what happened, and he was asked, "Are these young men not always going in and out of the hall, what drew your eye on this occasion?"

'And he said, "Well, there were a number of Sinn Féiners there."

'And he was asked, "Aren't there always a few Sinn Féiners?"

'And he eventually said, "Well, we didn't see any trees!"

'So that drew a bit of laughter. They got sent to prison anyway. But a month later, 100 people turned up in Menlough with horses and ploughs to plough the farms. It was springtime, you see, and these young men would normally be around to do the work, and all this local support was here for them.

'Fr Burke was the local priest, and he violently opposed Sinn Féin. He would preach and preach about it, and one person said Fr Burke had two Gods – God himself and John Bull. The priest here in Mountbellew was also against Sinn Féin. A man called Sean O'Neill was working here – he was involved in the IRB and Sinn Féin. He was working in the local shop. The local parish were going to put on a play called *The West's Awake*, and the priest refused him.

Fr Burke was the local priest, and he violently opposed Sinn Féin. He would preach and preach about it, and one person said Fr Burke had two Gods – God himself and John Bull.

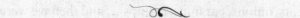

Sean O'Neill went to the priest and asked why. "We're all practising Catholics, we come down here and play billiards, this is the parish hall," he said.

But the priest refused to budge, and Sean O'Neill said, "You know what, a few weeks ago you let a travelling show in here, none of them went into the church and it was a load of smut, and you never criticised them."

So eventually the priest let them in, even though Sean O'Neill said they would go into the hall anyway!

'My mother's maiden name was Mellody; it's a very rare east Galway name. The Mellodys were in Guilka at least 200 years. The house where my mother grew up was a thatched house, built before 1838. Her mother was Anne Reynolds, who came from Killererin parish, and her father was from Abbeyknockmoy. It was an arranged marriage. There was a difference in years between my grandmother and grandfather that would have been typical of the area. He was born in 1880, and she was born in 1899. Men didn't get married in their twenties because they had to wait until they were more eligible and had the farm. So the love of his life when he was younger wouldn't wait around for him to get the farm!

'East Galway farming then consisted of spuds, carrots, onions, parsnips, turnips ... and then we were delighted when the new spuds came in. I remember as a kid, you'd have these watery spuds, and then the new spuds coming in and being so tasty, but digging potatoes was back-breaking work. Horses were the mainstay and most people kept a pig. The pigs were great recyclers and the banbh (or young pigs) were great for helping to pay the rent. I remember going out as a child to make sure the sow didn't eat her own banbhs.

'Growing up we still retained a little bit of the Irish language. In 1921 and 1922, the roll books of the local primary school were all in English, and then soon after the Free State came into being all the names would be there in Irish. That transition was incredible. Growing up, I never heard a sentence of Irish being spoken by anyone in the area. My grandmother on my dad's side lived with us, and she died when I was three. My grandmother on my mother's side, Anne Reynolds, died when I was 13. That's the sad thing – we were a Gaeltacht but, because of emigration, the language kind of died out. But we kept the residual: we always ate *prátaí* and drank *tae*!

> That's the sad thing – we were a Gaeltacht but, because of emigration, the language kind of died out. But we kept the residual: we always ate prátaí and drank tae!

'Anne Reynolds' sister-in-law has an interesting
connection; she was Kate Curley, the same surname
as myself. Kate had a sister Mary and she married
in Lackagh, close to Galway city. Her husband was
John O'Hanlon, and during the War of Independence
he was involved in the IRA. In October 1920 he
was on the run, and he came to visit his family.
He had two young children, and they heard the
sounds of a convoy. So they knew the Black and
Tans were coming. What they didn't know was that
the Black and Tans had already surrounded the
house. John tried to escape, he went out the back
door, and they heard a shot. The front door was
broken down and the Black and Tans came in and
intimidated the family, looking for John. Of course
his wife Mary said that he wasn't there, that she
didn't know where he was. They left eventually, and
Mary locked up the house and they went to bed.
When she got up the next morning and opened the
shutters of the house, there was John, splayed in a
crucified shape. They had shot him, taken his pipe
and left it on his chest, and left his corpse there.
Mary's brother-in-law was my grand-uncle, my
grandmother's brother, Malachy Reynolds. When
they had the funeral arranged, in Lackagh, the local
RIC came to them and said, "You've got to change
the mass time, it's going to be attacked." So they
changed it to an hour earlier and had just got the

body in the ground and next thing a convoy of
Black and Tans arrived, shots were fired and people
harassed.

When they had the funeral arranged,
in Lackagh, the local RIC came to them
and said, "You've got to change the mass
time, it's going to be attacked."

'I remember hearing stories of the Black and Tans
tying people to the back of their trucks by their feet
and dragging them along. The roads at that time were
obviously coarse sanded roads, so you can imagine
the damage that was done. That was common. There's

Martin Curley with his sister, Mary, and
her daughter, Catherine. Martin's children,
Carmel and Paddy, are in front.

a bridge near where I grew up that would have been a
vital cog in coming and going from the area, and the
Black and Tans made an attempt to bomb that bridge
so that the local IRA men wouldn't have access.
My mother's people, the Reynoldses, were close to
Tuam, and they would often hear the Black and Tans
coming when they were in the fields, and when they
did they would take pot shots at innocent people and
often killed them, so my mother's relations would
have to just get down and hide every time they heard
them coming.

> They would often hear the
> Black and Tans coming when they
> were in the fields, and when they did
> they would take pot shots at innocent
> people and often killed them.

'I was born in 1966. My parents married later
in life, so they grew up hearing all of these stories
and passing them along to us. When you think about
what they and their grandparents grew up with, not
only political things but the great influenza pandemic
too. We discovered another cousin recently, named
Elizabeth. Her grandmother, Ellen Curley, was
my father's aunt. When I contacted my cousins in
America and asked if they heard of this family, none

of them had. Ellen had siblings in New York, so on my Curley side, only two of my grandfather Patrick's siblings stayed in Ireland. The rest went to America but they were close enough to each other. As a kid, I remember in early December getting these magical Christmas cards from America. Something about the American stamps, with the address on a label, the luxury of the envelope, it was magical! They would come to visit in the 1960s and 1970s, but nobody knew about Ellen's family. Ellen had died in 1918 of the flu.

'Although most of my grandfather Patrick's siblings had gone to America, by the 1930s that route had been choked off by the Great Depression. So when the next generation, my father's siblings, were of age, England was the destination of choice. Two of them, Julia and Mary, emigrated just before the Second World War. They went with a local neighbour, so three Irish girls headed off to London from a small thatched cottage in Ireland. The following year, when the war arrived, they got transferred with their work to Warrington and settled down there.

'My aunt Mary married Ed Moran; he grew up in Warrington, but both of his parents are Irish. Warrington is about 25 per cent Galway; it's about 40 per cent Irish but with a huge Galway population. Mary came home to Ireland with her husband for a visit in 1948, and over the years returned frequently.

'My aunt Bridgie also went to England, as did my uncle Paddy. Uncle Jimmy went out for a while and then came back. I went over for a visit and I was chatting to my cousin Catherine. We went to pick up her daughter Ruth from the stables where she was riding. Catherine loved horses, and Ruth carried on that tradition. Catherine told me that inside those stables her mother told her a story about her grandfather, also my grandfather, Patrick. He had been a migrant worker, as many people were. He talked to Mary, his daughter, about being in a barn when a shot was fired, and how the bullets were still in the wall. It turned out to be the same barn where her daughter and granddaughter went to horse ride!'

16

Sean O'Keeffe

THE QUIET MEN

'There were shots fired over his coffin.
I wasn't expecting it! My mother was still
alive then and she was very proud of him.'

That is the memory Brigid Dillon has of her father Sean O'Keeffe's funeral in 1966. Sean was a quartermaster of the mid-Clare brigade in the Irish Volunteers during the War of Independence. He has contributed extensively to the Bureau of Military History that organised the taking of the witness statements which are now housed in the Military Archives. In one witness statement, he recounts how they planned one of their attacks.

About the middle of July 1919, I represented the 1st Battalion at a meeting of the Mid Clare Brigade Council held in the Clare Hotel in Ennis.

Frank Barrett presided. It was agreed to that an attempt should be made to capture the R.I.C. hut at Inch which was occupied by a sergeant and four constables. Each policeman, of course, was armed with a carbine and a revolver. It was the practice at this station to send out a patrol of two men every night and it was decided at the meeting that this patrol should be held up and disarmed as it was returning back to barracks at a point along the road 300 yards or so from that building. With the disarming of the patrol accomplished, two Volunteers should then proceed to the barracks, knock at the door and, when it opened, rush the place, supported by other men who would be lying conveniently outside.

Brigid tells me that her father was one of nine children. 'He was born in 1889 on a small farm in Carrowhill, Crusheen. His brother Michael had the farm. My father was the eldest and Michael was next. My father had other ways of living so Michael had the farm. Michael married Maisie O'Halloran and they settled there. They had four children: one was a priest, Fr Jack O'Keeffe. Then there was Cronin O'Keeffe, who runs the farm now, and a brother Anthony, who worked as head of forestry in Mayo, and they had a daughter May, or Mary.

'My father did work on the farm because his father died young, so he had to come back and help his mother run the farm, and then after a few years he got a job as a postman in the area. He went into the building trade for a while, serving his time with a firm of stonemasons. While there he came in contact with men in the Fenian movement. He didn't speak much about that sort of stuff. All the O'Keeffes were quiet men, gentle men, that generation. My father himself in later years, when I got to know him better, he was a great step dancer and we would have social gatherings in the house in Ard na Gréine. He would do lilting, he had a great sense of humour, and he was a people person. He had a lot of friends; he'd go down to the local pub in Ennis – they called it The Graveyard, because it was next to the abbey!'

Sean married Bridget Shannon from Cranny in west Clare. 'She had been nursing in Brighton in England, and she came back to Ireland around the time of the Civil War. She was nursing in the hospital in Ennis. She couldn't get involved in any activity in the IRA but she was a big sympathiser. The nurses were great; they would help however they could. I think that's how my parents met. When I was growing up, my father never spoke at all about that era. A lot of his friends were on the opposite side during the Civil War.

'My mother and father ran a post office, Clonmore Road post office in Ard na Gréine, and I ran it after them. I was the only one still living in Ireland later in my father's life, and he would drive me out to the farm, when I was 16 or 17. I used to love going out. I used to stay in the house with my uncle's wife Maisie, my father's sister-in-law. I remember she used to make lovely rice pudding! My father would go out to the farm to his brother; they were very close. I'd go out looking for them a couple of hours later and they would be sitting down having their *seanchas* or chat. It was lovely. I used to love going out there. I didn't help on the farm – they used to keep me away from all that!

'We were kept away from the town as young people. Myself and my parents went to mass every morning at seven o'clock in the Friary. My father had the car – he was in the Land Commission at this stage. In those days you'd have to fast before mass, from twelve o'clock the night before. Their faith meant a lot to them. When we were young we said the rosary every night: we had to go down on our knees and say the whole thing! We'd all be giggling and my father would get annoyed and have to get up and walk away.

> When we were young we said the rosary every night: we had to go down on our knees and say the whole thing! We'd all be giggling and my father would get annoyed and have to get up and walk away.

'My father never spoke about the Civil War. My mother did, though; she would tell us stories, including one about how my father went on hunger strike while in prison. Prisoners would write poetry or draw little pictures, and there was a painting drawn of my father when he was on hunger strike, and he was very gaunt-looking. My mother hated it and gave it away to one of the family. During the Civil War my father was on the run and had to hide out in safe houses. There was one time he stayed with teachers and they gave him food and hid him – but they would have both lost their jobs if they had been found out.

> During the Civil War my father was on the run and had to hide out in safe houses. There was one time he stayed with teachers and they gave him food and hid him – but they would have both lost their jobs if they had been found out.

'I was married in 1961. I remember my wedding day well. My father was sick, so my very good friend and cousin, Colonel Tom McNamara, gave me away. Tom came from Crusheen, so the O'Keeffes and the McNamaras had a big connection there. He was aide-de-camp to President de Valera. We were married in

St Joseph's church in Limerick, and we went to Achill island for our honeymoon. We stayed in the Mulranny hotel. It was gorgeous – we were in a different world. We had four children. The eldest was Peter, then Tom, then Claire and then John. I have eight grandchildren and four great-grandchildren.

'My mother really looked after my father when he was sick. He was very healthy and very strong for most of their lives; he was a great provider and he could boil a kettle! That was something. He was wonderful. He would go off to the bog with his friends and cut the turf and arrange to bring it home in a big lorry. In Ard na Gréine, we had a big shed, and I remember the turf being packed up in big stacks. He was great in the garden as well: he would grow all our vegetables.

'My father worked in the Land Commission all his life, until he retired. He had an IRA pension. He had medals and all. I have a photo of him walking over a bridge wearing his medals – that was shortly before he died. They were celebrating 50 years since 1916, so there was a memorial erected in Ennis. It's still there. It's in Irish, there's no personal information or anything, it's just commemorating it.'

When Sean O'Keeffe died on 3 July 1966 he had a huge funeral. 'We didn't have any undertakers back then, so it was from the house in Ard na Gréine. It would be a friend or a neighbour that would lay the person out then. A nurse called Biddy Kinnane did it for my father.

We didn't have any undertakers
back then, so it was from the house
in Ard na Gréine. It would be a friend
or a neighbour that would lay the
person out then.

'He was one that never looked for any type of praise; he would always give it to somebody else. He was never one for blowing his own trumpet. There were shots fired over his coffin. I wasn't expecting it! My mother was still alive then and she was very

Sean O'Keeffe, far left, during celebrations for the fiftieth anniversary of the 1916 Rising.

proud of him. She would be the one who told the stories about him. She lived until 1994; she was 93 when she died. My father died suddenly. He died in the garden, listening to a match on the radio. He always smoked a pipe. It was the Munster final, I think, which was a big match, and it was very exciting. I was gone to Lahinch with three of my children and some of their friends. My husband Tom had stayed to listen to the match. The next thing my father dropped dead, and the pipe fell out of his mouth and he was gone. A beautiful way to go, really. Although my mother went to pieces then; it was very hard on her.

'I took over the post office in 1974. I was living in Kincora Park here in the town. Three of my children were born there, in Kincora Park, and then we bought the house I was born in from my mother, Ard na Gréine. It was lovely to live there, even though I did love the house I was living in at the time. My boys went to boarding school up in St Flannan's College and Claire went to the Sisters of Mercy in Kinvara.

'My father had a brother, Tom, who emigrated to Wisconsin; he had two children. He worked in the office in the railway, and he was very, very quiet and gentle. His daughter was a nurse and she would tell us about him. Another brother, Dan O'Keeffe, he drove the west Clare railway, and he never married. I really didn't know him but he was supposed to be a lovely man, and great fun. He drove the steam engine from Clare to Galway. I went once or twice on the steam train to Lahinch – it was great craic. We used to have an excursion on a Sunday, and the train would break down. Do you know the song 'Are You Right There, Michael, Are You Right?' My father was a wonderful singer, he would do the lilting because they had no instruments. He was a beautiful step dancer as well.

'My husband Tom is dead now; he died in 1990. He was 68. There was 14 years between himself and myself. I was 23 or 24 when I was married. A lot of girls back then married older men.

'They always thought Tom was going to be a priest, because he was nearly 40 when he got married, you know. There was nine in his family. He was a very gentle man as well, like my father. He never raised a hand to anyone.'

17

Anne Keogh

A FENIAN FAMILY

'Behind the false back of the
wardrobe there was a space where
you could hide a man or hide guns.'

When Anne Keogh (née Somers) was a little girl, Britain's Queen Victoria visited Dún Laoghaire. The six-year-old, born in 1894, was determined to see the queen. The story is taken up by her granddaughters, Mimi and Leah, whom I interviewed together on Zoom. A wonderful quirk of their close relationship and shared history is that they finish each other's sentences. Here, their chat appears as a single voice.

'Our nana talked about that trip a lot; she was very specific about it. She came from a family that was originally from Wexford, a very republican family, very rebellious. She wanted to go and see the queen and her mother couldn't take her because she had a few small children at home to look after. So she asked her uncle – his name was Willie Ford. He didn't want to do it, obviously: he wouldn't be seen dead going to see Queen Victoria. But my nana was dying to go and she bought a Union Jack, and her mother *made* Willie bring her. He walked behind her, way behind her, because he didn't want to be seen with someone who had a Union Jack!

> He walked behind her, way behind her, because he didn't want to be seen with someone who had a Union Jack!

'But even as a little girl, my nana was so disappointed because she said Queen Victoria was old and fat and ugly! She told us, "She was like an aul wan that you'd see sitting on the steps selling fish!" She had imagined a young and beautiful queen, I suppose, so she was very disappointed. But she remembered it all so well due to the fight with her mother and uncle. That's the earliest memory she had.

'Her father was an alcoholic and was asked to leave the house by her mother, so she was left with four girls then. They had to take people into the house, lodgers, as a lot of people did in Bray at the time. Their house was on the Meath Road, called Coolgreaney, which was named after where her great-grandfather had come from. He was one of the people who had been evicted in the 1887 Coolgreaney evictions.

'A neighbour across the road took in lodgers too, for the College of Surgeons. They would have come from India. Obviously they would be talking to the girls – the girls were very pretty so the doctors would stop and chat with them and have them over for evenings of song and chat. They were seen walking on the beach with them and it went round the town.

'Next thing the parish priest called to my great-grandmother and said, "Do you realise that your daughters have been seen fraternising with men from a different continent?"

'So our great-grandmother ran him and said, "How dare you call here and suggest anything bad is going on just because your mind is bad. I have complete trust in my girls."

'Apparently she was quite a scary lady and I like that, because a lot of women were intimidated by the Catholic Church back then, but she wasn't.

'My great-grandmother was born Elizabeth Anne Ford and when she married she was Elizabeth Somers. Our family was known as being republican, or Fenians as they were called back then. She remembered the run-up to 1916. She said she knew there was something going on; there was an atmosphere about the house in Coolgreaney and quite a lot of young men around the house. We're not sure but we think Éamonn Ceannt might have been one of them.

'They were all in the house and Mother Somers said to the girls, "Go and get the simnel cake and give it to these guys before they leave."

'And the girls replied, "No, they can't have it, it's Good Friday, we're fasting today."

'But Granny Somers told them to give it to them, and some ham as well, and that's when the girls knew there was something big about to happen, and that the guys might never come back. It would have been their last supper.

'When Elizabeth was very young, there was only one other person in the village her own age. That was the doctor's daughter, and she had a tutor, and her parents didn't want her to be spoiled. So Elizabeth got an education too, courtesy of the doctor's daughter!

'During the First World War, Elizabeth's four girls used to do a lot of embroidery and lace work and they always had lovely pretty collars on their dresses. And when they went out, the neighbours, who were pro-British, would go "German gold, German gold" under their breath – in other words,

"You got the clothes from the Germans!" Whereas the truth was that Elizabeth was running a boarding house, she had people there, they were all working, so there was some money coming in and they could afford all this.

'Anne Elizabeth was the eldest, then Eileen, Kathleen, and Mae was the youngest. Tragically, Kathleen died when she was 20, in 1918, she had TB. That was the big killer in those days. I have a card from Mabel FitzGerald to Mother Somers, commiserating with her on Kathleen's death. Mabel was the wife of Desmond FitzGerald and mother of Taoiseach Garret FitzGerald. From 1918 to '21 she was on the Cumann na mBan executive council. She took part in the 1916 Easter Rising and was also active in the War of Independence. She was against the treaty, while her husband took the pro-treaty stance.

'The War of Independence was quite interesting because they were good friends of Mabel and Desmond FitzGerald, both of whom were on the run for different reasons. My grandmother and her sisters and my great-grandmother lived on Loreto Terrace in Bray at the time, and, however it happened, when Mabel and Desmond were on the run, young Desmond and his brother Garret were sent down to stay with Mother Somers for a while.

'Mabel and our auntie Mae were very good friends. Mabel was George Bernard Shaw's secretary.

My nana met him once when he called to the house looking for Mabel. He knew that she lived in Bray somewhere but wasn't sure where. So he called to the house and nana walked him around to Thomond Avenue. They didn't talk the whole way; she didn't know what to say to him and he said nothing to her! But she loved the fact that she met George Bernard Shaw. The Somers minded the FitzGerald kids for a few months, one long stint I think. The FitzGerald children also had a governess.

'My great-grandmother had quite a big house on the Meath Road. There was a landing on the second-from-the-top storey, and it had an absolutely enormous wardrobe on it that had a false back. Behind the false back there was a space where you could hide a man or hide guns. This was well known in their family, but it wouldn't have been known anywhere else. One night the Black and Tans arrived, and Mother Somers went ballistic; they were all very upset because they were in bed at the time, all young girls, you know. The Black and Tans pulled them out of their beds and were really rough with them. There was a British officer who walked in and gave out to the Black and Tans for mishandling young women! So they didn't search the house in the end.

'Our nana fell in love with one of the boarders in the house, Frank Kinsella. He was older than her but he fancied her right from the start. He did many jobs, his main one being a commercial traveller for jewellery. He was a bibliophile, he collected books; Leah has a fabulous library in her house because of it.

> The Black and Tans pulled them out of
> their beds and were really rough with
> them. There was a British officer who
> walked in and gave out to the Black and
> Tans for mishandling young women!

'She was very disappointed because on her twenty-first birthday he gave her an umbrella with a gold handle on it, and she thought it was hideous. It made her feel like an old person. She thought it was the weirdest present ever, and then a couple of years later she married him! He used to give her gold, a gold ring or whatever, for every single birthday, and then once they got married he never gave her gold again. Her wedding dress was absolutely beautiful, and she had a veil too, both handmade by herself and her sisters.

'She got married at 23 and had three children and then, tragically, Frank died from TB at the age of 30. She was widowed for 73 years and she never married again. Frank had got the "black flu", and recovered from it, and then got TB and died.

'Nana moved back to Bray from Dundrum, to her

mother, and again the priest came down and said, "With no father around, we better take the three kids from you and look after them, because you won't be able to look after them yourself."

'And again, herself and her mother said, "You will take these children over our dead bodies." Thank God, because God knows what would have happened to them.

'Then my widowed grandmother made a life-changing decision. She decided to go to art college, which was unheard of in those days, especially being 30 with three small children. She went to art college in Dundrum, and she became an art teacher. She got work in the local technical school, teaching art and design and technical drawing, and she didn't stop working until she was 83 years of age! And that is how she brought up her kids as a single mother. I think it's absolutely amazing. She was living with her mother after her husband died but then one of her sisters moved home too and so nana moved out. She just wanted to get away and have her independence. She managed to buy an old house with broken floorboards for 350 pounds. She fixed it up over the years and Leah is still living there.

'Nana always said, "I was very sad when Frank died, but I never would have had the life I did have if he hadn't died." She meant that if he had lived, she wouldn't have gone to college and become an art student, and she wouldn't have met all the interesting people she did meet doing art. She always said, "Although I missed him, and I was sad, I had a great life *because* he died." She understood that if she was still married, she would have had more children and stayed at home as a housewife.

'She did meet very interesting people in art college; she would have known quite a lot of younger people, mostly upper-class people, who went to art college in those days. She would have known Evie Hone, and Sean Keating was one of her teachers. My nana was very conservative in many ways and religious, but when she was in art college she saw it all. She would go in with her sandwiches and her pack, because she wouldn't be able to afford to go out for lunch or anything like that, and some of the girls would come in and they were all young and studenty and bohemian, and she wasn't, she was a mother of three. She would end up giving away her sandwiches to her fellow students because they were all starving! That's why when one of the students painted a picture of Evie Hone, she gave it to Nana and said, "Maybe someday it will be worth something, and it will pay you back for all the sandwiches!" We still have that painting. It's a lovely thing to have.

'Our nana taught until she retired at 83. She retired from the school first, and then taught embroidery at nighttime; the last class she ever taught was when she was 98, and it was in the Bank of Ireland exhibition centre on Baggot Street. It was on embroidery, she was invited in to do it.

> She retired from the school first, and then taught embroidery at nighttime; the last class she ever taught was when she was 98, and it was in the Bank of Ireland exhibition centre on Baggot Street.

'Nana had three children: our mother, Kathleen, and two sons, Brian and Frankie. A lot of people in the town of Bray would have known our mother very well. She was always a community activist, part of the Bray Youth Council, and she started a drugs awareness programme before people even thought about it. She was in the Bray Literary Innovation Society, the Historical Society and the Tidy Towns, did some acting, and worked with Travellers. People always asked her would she become a politician but she never wanted that; she would have been compromised then. Our mum lived in the house that our grandmother bought on Alexander Terrace and this is where Leah has made her home.

'Our parents had seven children: Paul, Rory, Ruth, Darragh, Leah, Mark and Mimi. Our father died in 1976 when I was 12. He died young.

'Here's a lovely story! When Nana was 99 and Eileen was 97 and Mae was 95, we had a party in the house on the Meath Road for them to celebrate their birthdays. Eileen was in a wheelchair at that stage, and a lover of whiskey, Mae was the good-time girl, and Nana was the sensible one. It was a Saturday afternoon, and that day *The Irish Times* had a feature on a man called Seán Lester who had been secretary general of the League of Nations. It turned out that all three women knew him in their youth and had had a crush on him. Now in their nineties, they had a fight about which of them he liked the most!

'Mae said, "Well, he *always* liked me, I had some great times with him", to which Eileen replied, "I think he liked *me* just as much!"

'But Nana was having none of it. "They don't know what they're talking about," she said, "*I* was his favourite."

'It was so funny, they were like teenagers! I thought it was absolutely fascinating seeing these three old ladies giggling and laughing and being jealous of each other!

'When Nana was turning 99, we said, "We should probably organise a party now, just in case!" We could say that sort of thing to her – she was very straightforward. But she said, "No, no, I don't want a big birthday for my ninety-ninth, I want a proper one for my hundredth."

'So we said we would go down to Coolgreaney, in Wexford, where her mother was from, and we arranged a bus. But we didn't tell her that we were also organising another party for all her friends in Bray.

'"Do you think this is a good idea," my brother Paul said, "to have a surprise party for a 100-year-old? We could kill her!"

"Sure won't she die happy!" I replied.'

Nana had a great sense of humour and made up names for her grandchildren. She called one of them 'blotting paper', she called Mimi 'the simple, homey one' and she once gave Leah an article titled 'Plain Girls Too Can Get Their Man'!

On Saturdays or Sundays she used to teach Mimi how to talk to a man. 'She would say, "If a man says, 'The First World War was caused by the Turkish', don't go 'Don't be ridiculous, you silly man'. Instead say, 'Really, dear?'" But it was so funny because she would never have done that in a million years! She was just trying to teach me how to flirt. I think she was enjoying it.

'My grandmother and her sisters were interesting people. Her sister Eileen had ten children, one of whom is one of Ireland's best known artists, Brian Bourke. And Fergus Bourke, who was a well-known photographer, he did all the photography for the Abbey and for Edna O'Brien's books. Mae had a son called Rory Breslin, who was a famous sculptor.

'Nana never went to funerals. The first funeral she was at in years was her sister Mae's. She always said that she had a really strong faith, but because she went to so many funerals when she was young, she eventually decided not to go to any more. "I will be good to people when they're alive," she said.

'When she went to auntie Mae's funeral I asked her about it. "You haven't been to a funeral in years, not my father's, not your grandson's. Why auntie Mae?"

'"I figure it's my turn next," she replied, "and I'd love to see what it is all about." And that is what she meant, she was researching!

'We had a lot of laughs together, but what I loved most about her was her self-sufficiency and her inner strength. In Ireland, it is unheard of not to go to funerals – people were always so shocked to hear she didn't. That one move alone taught us that we don't have to do everything we are expected to. Nana died on the 12th of June 1997, aged 103.'

In Ireland, it is unheard of not to go to funerals – people were always so shocked to hear she didn't. That one move alone taught us that we don't have to do everything we are expected to.

18

Eugene O'Sullivan

CUTTING THE TURF

'They used to practise and train.
They'd be out waiting all night long
for the lorries to come. They used to
get the poor cattle up out of their
beds, and they would lie down there
instead, because it would be warm!'

Kitty Sheahan (née O'Sullivan) is 90 years old and she's telling me about her father Eugene O'Sullivan's involvement in the IRA. 'My father was 22 in 1916 and he lived in the parish of Dromanig, Tullylease in County Cork. He joined the Irish Volunteers and was in the 4th Battalion. Their job was to walk around the village and keep an eye out, and on Good Friday in 1916 they walked to Barley Hill Bridge, which was about eight miles away. They were expecting guns to come in that day on

Eugene O'Sullivan and Molly Walsh
married in Broadford, County Limerick,
6 February 1926.

a German cargo ship, the *Aud*, but the Royal Navy had intercepted it and so there were no guns for the Volunteers. The ship was carrying more than 20,000 weapons and its capture led to the arrest of Roger Casement.

'The battalion used to practise and train. They'd be out waiting all night long for the lorries to come. They used to get the poor cattle up out of their beds, and they would lie down there instead, because it would be warm! I'm sure they had coats and that, but it would have been a tough auld time.

'Dad was at home one day in the kitchen, and next thing a lorry pulled up outside the door, with soldiers in it, and there was a man who came in and said to my grandmother, "Hello, mother, have you seen your son lately?" And she said, "No, I haven't seen my son in a month." But Dad and his friend were in the back room, with the door half open, and the friend wanted to hop out the window. That would have got them shot straight away though, from the lorry. But the soldiers didn't search the house at all: they went away again. They were looking for my father and his friend – they had an idea that they were there, but they didn't search. They had a list of names, I think, and they knew who was involved. They probably wanted information. This was my grandmother's house, before my father got married.

'Another night they were looking for him and they found him, I think they gave him a few pucks and a few belts. They were looking for Eugene O'Sullivan, but he gave his name as Eugene Bigley, which was his mother's name. The IRA used to cut down a couple of feet into the road, so the lorries couldn't pass –

that was something they did a lot. My father wasn't necessarily a wanted man but I suppose a lot of his crowd were. My grandfather wasn't involved at all.

The IRA used to cut down a couple of
feet into the road, so the lorries couldn't
pass – that was something they did a lot.

'I have two brothers, neither of them living, and two sisters, both of them living. And then myself. My father wasn't married until 1926, which was ten years after the Rising.

'Eugene O'Sullivan and Molly Walsh had six living children, but I think maybe eight in total: they lost a couple. Their wedding was in Broadford, County Limerick. She just had a friend as a bridesmaid, and Dad had his friend there too. My mother had no sisters, only brothers, and my dad had no family, so they were their witnesses. They went to Cork for a day and a night on their honeymoon and I have their wedding photo at home.

'My father worked on the roads for the council, and my mother was a dressmaker. She made all of our clothes, school clothes and sheets and everything. It was a lot of work, and she did all the baking and all as well. A very busy woman.

My mother was a dressmaker. She
made all of our clothes, school clothes
and sheets and everything. It was a
lot of work, and she did all the
baking and all as well.

'My father was a very intelligent man and himself
and my mother were great, they educated us all. He
went to the bog, and he grew potatoes, they kept a
few cows, and he was good with wood too: he made
our table and dressers and a few cupboards. My
brothers would help on the bog as well: it was a big
job. I went once or twice but it was a long way away.
They would go by pony and cart, but one brother
wouldn't have the patience and he would go on his
bike. It was a big job with lots of steps: you'd have
to cut it and dry it, and when it was dried they'd
have to bring it from the middle of the bog out to the
road, and then bring it all home. They would keep at
it until they had a rake of it at home.

'We had no electricity or running water – we
just had lamps and candles. We used to go up to
the spring well and get water to make tea and all,
and to do all the washing-up. It was a tough life. We
were way out in the country. We'd go shopping in
the town: we'd bring eggs in from our hen, and we'd

sell the eggs in town and be able to buy some of the messages then.

> We'd go shopping in the town: we'd
> bring eggs in from our hen, and we'd sell
> the eggs in town and be able to
> buy some of the messages then.

'We walked a mile and a half to school every day; we'd be there from half nine till probably three o'clock. This was during the Second World War. We had two teachers, one of them was called "the master". We had a radio but no television; we would play hurling and football and all and go to mass and devotions and that.

'My father was still on the roads; he worked on the roads until he retired. I had great parents – they worked so hard. Mum did all the cooking and cleaning and ironing and all these things; when I got bigger I would help with ironing and that. We got to go to secondary school as well and got an education.

'When we were young I remember that when somebody died who had been in the IRA, there would always be a firing party, where they would fire up into the air, and Dad would often be in the firing squad. He never went to prison – he was lucky. I remember a young boy from the parish who hadn't been so lucky. The Black and Tans would drive by in lorries and shoot at anybody they wanted, and he was shot. They shot people all the time. My father had a good few medals for taking part in the War of Independence. All the Volunteers had to go to Dublin to be interviewed for the military pensions given by the new Free State government for those who had fought in 1916 and the War of Independence.

When we were young I remember that when somebody died who had been in the IRA, there would always be a firing party, where they would fire up into the air.

'When I left school I got a scholarship to go on and become a cheesemaker. I was trained in Freemount. I trained there for the summer until October, and then an inspector came from the Department of Agriculture and he gave me a test, and I got a cert that qualified me to work. That was 1950.

I worked for a creamery then and made cheddar cheese. It's a lot more modern now; it was basic but hard work back then. I never make cheese now – you'd have to have rennet and all to put into the milk and get it to set. You'd have to separate the whey and curds, and it would be left for months in moulds, and then it would be cut up months later. It was mainly cheddar back then; now there are other cheeses made, not just cheddar.

'I met my husband working at the creamery. He was a cheesemaker too. His name was Denis Sheahan. He came from about five miles down the country, he loved GAA and he never drank or smoked. We got married on the 4th of February 1967. We had our honeymoon in London; Denis had a sister and a couple of brothers over there, so it only cost us the flights. We were over for a week. I knew him for a while before we got married – he was working beside me for a good bit before anything happened! We were just co-workers. He had a car, which helped a bit, but not really! We were in a flat for a while, and then we bought the house we are still living in, on Charleville Road, Newmarket. I have one girl, Maura, and two grandchildren, two lovely girls.

'I remember back when my grandmother died, there happened to be a "pattern" on in Tullylease at the time. We used to always get the day off school when the "pattern" was on.

'We would come with our shillings and be delighted to be out. That night there would be a big dance, and loads of people would come, and we would pray the rounds. St Benjamin is our patron saint – loads of people around had that name, or Ben. We would always have the Passion then, on the 18th of February. My grandmother died around then, and I remember there was no dance that night. It was out of respect; she lived down in the village.

'My dad, when he was small, he fell into the open fire; his face was burned. My grandmother would get up at dawn, and she went and prayed 21 rounds for him. On the twentieth morning his first eye was open, and on the twenty-first morning his second eye was open, and he never had a mark. He recovered totally. A lot of people would pray rounds then, for Our Lady and for St Ben. There was a big concrete stone down in one of the fields, with a mark down the middle of it, and people would go there, and it was great for headaches. There's an abbey down in the village of Tullylease, with a burial ground, and lots of stories about it.

> A lot of people would pray rounds then, for Our Lady and for St Ben. There was a big concrete stone down in one of the fields, with a mark down the middle of it, and people would go there, and it was great for headaches.

'Ireland today is very different to the Ireland I grew up in. It's better, of course, they have so much that we didn't have, didn't even know about. We would have the same dinner every night, bacon and cabbage and turnip and, on occasion, a stew. Santy would come at Christmas; we would do up the house with holly and paper hangings, and candles lighting. There was mass on Christmas Day. Santy would have come in the meantime, of course, maybe with a teddy or a dolly or a ball for the boys or something. They were very simple days; people didn't have the money. They were paid by the week. They managed to educate every one of us, though – they were just great. My father had a good job but a lot of people had to just depend on the farming. We had more than some of the neighbours.

'My father died in 1976; he was 82. My mother was only 69 when she died. My brother who was the first-born, he died when he was only 67 of a massive heart attack. He left a young family of six children and his wife. I'm the longest living of them all. I've two sisters still alive but they're younger than me.'

19

The Healy Brothers

CHILDREN AT THE EUCHARISTIC CONGRESS

'The story goes in the family that Myles
na gCopaleen's *The Third Policeman* was
based on our uncle Frank! According to
Flann anyway.'

It was Saturday, 25 June 1932, when Sara and
Michael Healy drove from their home in Lobinstown
in County Meath to Dublin's Phoenix Park to
celebrate Children's Day at the Eucharistic Congress.
They brought their two children, Ethna and Colm. 'I
remember it was a terribly hot summer's day. There
was no Fanta or Coke or lemonade in those days but
there were boy scouts going around with barrels of

buttermilk. If you were thirsty, you went up to a boy scout and he gave you a scoop of buttermilk!

'There were huge crowds there and the papal legate, Cardinal Lorenzo Lauri, officiated as the pope didn't travel in those days. And at the end of the mass our parents brought us to the zoo! Of course, this was fantastic! My brother was four and I was six, and whenever anyone asked him what he saw at the Eucharistic Congress, he would say, "An elephant and a cardinal!"'

Whenever anyone asked him what he
saw at the Eucharistic Congress, he
would say, "An elephant and a cardinal!"'

I'm talking to Sr Ethna and her brother, Professor Des Swan, whose mother Sara was one of the nine children of Pat and Kathleen Healy, national school teachers in Shanballymore, in the parish of Doneraile.

Sr Ethna still remembers her paternal grandmother. 'My grandparents were from Carlinstown, near Kells. We used to go over in the car on a Sunday to see them. My grandmother, believe it or not, had a tobacco farm, of all things. She used to go up the hill and she would hear the car coming and she would race down! She had a little white bonnet and a pinafore. She died when she was about 96. She grew tobacco plants, and in those days everyone smoked. There was a tobacco factory in Dundalk then.'

'The Healys were a big family,' Des tells me, 'about nine children. The eldest was Elizabeth but she was known as Ban. She became a teacher and later went to live in Kent on her own, with her dog and her duck, at the mouth of the Thames. She wrote quite a bit, mainly articles for teaching journals. She had two children: one became an economist and one became a nurse.

> My grandmother, believe it or not,
> had a tobacco farm, of all things.
> She grew tobacco plants, and in
> those days everyone smoked.

'Then there was Sr Agnes, who became a Mercy nun in the convent in Dundalk, and we grew up in County Meath so we would have visited her quite a bit. She was kind of a favourite aunt of ours; I remember when I was in Donegal at 14 years of age and I ran out of money, and I wrote to her and she sent me half a crown in a matchbox! She was great. Augusta, or auntie Gus, she stayed on in the homeplace in Shanballymore, and she became a junior assistant mistress in the local school. She was married and had a great number of children, who are all scattered around now. She and her husband, Gus Farrell, had a pub in Shanballymore. It wasn't particularly respectable to them to have a pub back then, so they only opened it for one week in the year to keep their licence. They had two daughters; one became a teacher and one became a nurse.

'There were three boys, Des and Kevin and Cormac. When Kevin died, his brother Des, who was a priest, came back to mind his kids for him – they were still young. Des passed away about seven years later. Cormac was a farmer. He too passed away, so there is nobody left in the house and pub in Shanballymore, where my mother and her family grew up.

> It wasn't particularly respectable to
> them to have a pub back then, so
> they only opened it for one week in
> the year to keep their licence.

'Then there were Frank and Sean, both very active in the old IRA. Sean was based in Cork, working by day as station master in the railway station, but involved in the IRA. He came home for Christmas in 1920, and he was celebrating with the whole family on St Stephen's Day when one of the sisters heard a noise outside and they realised they were about to be invaded by the Black and Tans. Sean and Frank made it out the back window, and ran through the fields and hid behind the church until the danger had passed.'

In his witness statement to the Bureau of Military History Sean described the raid, when two lorries of British soldiers arrived in Shanballymore.

They halted in front of our house, when the soldiers dismounted and rushed into the house. My sister Ina, who was a member of the local Cumann na mBan Company, observed the lorries approaching when they were within 100 yards of the house and apprised us of the fact. Without wasting a minute, we dashed out at the back door, scaled a wall, ran across the adjoining school-yard and hid in a recess at the back of the Church, where we remained until they withdrew. Being armed with an automatic pistol, I would have sold my life dearly if trapped. My father, mother and the other female members of the family were subjected to a severe cross-examination about the activities of the Sinn Féiners in the village apart from my brother and me. Ignorance was pleaded about everything in the nature of the political activities and the soldiers departed, stating that they would call again.

Frank also wrote an account of the raid and said, 'We seemed to be getting climatised [sic] to living an existence as hunted men.'

Des and Ethna's parents, Sara and Michael, were both teachers in the local school. They were paid quarterly, and on pay day they would make their way into Doneraile on the pony and trap to collect their salary. The couple were married in 1926 and Des tells me the story. 'My father was a teacher in County Meath; he was from a big family in Carranstown. Their grandmother spoke Irish, which was dying out in County Meath, in the Pale, at that time. He would remember her speaking Irish to her friends, and she would remember the Fenians, and Fenian activity in that area in the time after the 1798 rebellion – and which carried on for the best part of a century. One group of the croppies from County Wexford made their way up to County Meath, to a place called the hill of Raffin, and that was their last stand. That was where they fell. Seamus Heaney in one of his poems talks about the corn growing in the pockets where they lay. That is still remembered in that part of the country.

'We grew up about ten miles from there, near Slane in a place called Lobinstown. That was where my father taught. My parents met in 1925. Every national teacher was required to teach Irish, by the government, and as you can imagine, at that stage a lot of them had very little or no Irish at all. So they were all required to attend summer classes in Irish, to brush up what they had or to acquire what they needed. My father went to an Irish class in Youghal, County Cork, and this young lady was sitting beside him. They got talking, ended up engaged within three weeks, and married within a few more weeks! What happened before that was this: the parish priest was the manager of the school, and he put his head in the door one day and said to my father, "The numbers are going up, master, and we need a mistress! If you don't get one … I will!" So that was the background to my father heading to Youghal and coming back engaged. They met in August and they were married in September.'

My parents met in 1925. Every national teacher was required to teach Irish, by the government, and as you can imagine, at that stage a lot of them had very little or no Irish at all.

Sara was from Cork and had trained in Marlborough Street teacher training college in Dublin. 'It was during the War of Independence,' says Ethna. 'When the students went out on the streets, they were told that if there was a raid, they were to lie flat on the ground until the raid was over. My mother and another student were out somewhere near Stephen's Green one day and there was a raid. So they both fell flat onto the ground, and the other student said, "Oh if I'm shot my mother will kill me!"'

So they both fell flat onto the ground,
and the other student said, 'Oh if
I'm shot my mother will kill me!'

Sr Ethna recalls walking barefoot to school. 'We lived in the teachers' house half a mile from the school and we used to walk over there every day. In those days we didn't have any radio, television, mobiles. In our spare time all we would do was read, read, read! I remember the day they brought me up to the school and my mother knocked on the door and handed me in to her colleague. The teacher was sitting in her chair at the desk; I walked up, but there were a whole load of children's pictures on the wall and I stopped and looked at every picture on my way up to her! I remember that day quite well.'

After Ethna came Fr Colm, who was a parish priest, and then Leo. Ethna remembers Leo's arrival, the only child not to have been born at home. 'My father brought Colm and myself up to the nursing home in Dublin. I remember the room. There were two beds and two cots: one was a pink cot and one was a blue cot. I was dying for the pink cot with the little girl, but we got Leo instead in the blue cot!'

She also recalls the birth of her brother Des, on 9 February 1932, when 'three extraordinary things happened. First, my brother Desmond was born, then the parish priest died and the third extraordinary thing was that my father went for the milk because the snow was so bad! We couldn't believe it.

> There were two beds and two cots:
> one was a pink cot and one was a
> blue cot. I was dying for the pink cot
> with the little girl, but we got Leo
> instead in the blue cot!

'When Leo retired as a school principal he became a pioneer in aerial archaeology. He bought his own aeroplane, trained himself to fly, and also trained himself in photography, and he spent years flying, week in and week out, doing aerial photography. He would take photos of soil disturbances that wouldn't be visible from the ground, and from there you could track the pattern of habitation in a village. He was the first to do it, but now it's standard practice in archaeology, and there are thousands of his photos in the National Library. He passed away 20 years ago.

'Brendan was next. He passed away about ten years ago. He was in the airline industry and became

Dublin manager for Alitalia. He worked in Dublin airport and had his own plane too, which he flew quite a lot. Eventually he moved from that into auctioneering. Then there's myself. I have a PhD in psychology. I got an award for my PhD from America from the International Reading Association. I carried out a national survey of the reading standards of students in first year in second-level schools. I showed that about 15 per cent of kids who move from primary to secondary have a reading difficulty. Up to that time, the Department of Education would not admit this openly, but I was able to statistically prove it, if you like. They grudgingly admitted it then and started employing remedial teachers and learning support teachers. Gradually. So in fact, policy changed from then on.'

Des has written or contributed to ten books, and his thesis for his PhD in English Literature was on Patrick Kavanagh, whom he once met in a bookshop on Baggot Street. He was also the first Irish teacher in St Kilian's German School in Dublin in the 1950s. 'I taught there for about six or seven years, and I stayed longer than I should have because I loved the German food! They had a great dinner every day. I was spoiled in St Kilian's because I got on very well – it was a very personal and informal school. I taught English, Irish, Latin, Maths –

everything – and brought them all for Confessions every month.

> I stayed longer than I should have
> because I loved the German food!
> They had a great dinner every day.

'At one point, we moved from Leeson Park to Stillorgan Road, to a new building, and they wanted to have it blessed. So they asked the parish priest in Donnybrook would he bless the building, and he said, "On one condition – that no person is on the premises when I do so." Which I thought was very strange. So when it came to the time of the blessing of the building, all three of us teachers had to go to the pub until it was over! He was doing us a favour, I suppose!'

Des retired from his teaching career in UCD in 1997, where he held the chair of education, but he is still writing and lecturing. 'I've given presentations on Kavanagh as recently as a few months ago, in the U3A, which is the University of Third Age, online. Myself and my wife Mary have done presentations for them on Kavanagh's poetry, and on the psychology of poetry, and the connections between poetry and psychology.' Des and Mary have five children and 13 grandchildren.

So when it came to the time of the
blessing of the building, all
three of us teachers had to go to
the pub until it was over!

Ethna takes up the story to tell me about her only sister. 'Nuala was a nurse by profession and she was eight years younger than me. She died on Easter Monday 2020 and she had a very tough time for the week before Easter. I couldn't go to the funeral or to see her because of coronavirus. It was very frustrating. Her eldest daughter Aoife is fantastic: she looked after her when she was sick. Nuala was cremated, and when all this is over we will have a family get-together and a remembrance.

'Kevin was the youngest sibling. He was a priest for the Meath diocese, but left the priesthood and got married to a Belgian lady and they live in Belgium with their two kids, on the banks of the Meuse river. There are four of us still alive.'

However, it is Des's two uncles, Sean and Frank, who left a lasting mark on Irish nationalism. Frank became a garda and station sergeant in Dalkey, County Dublin and that is where he spent most of his working life. 'He was an odd character and the story goes in the family that Myles na gCopaleen's [aka Flann O'Brien/Brian O'Nolan] *The Third Policeman* was based on our uncle Frank! According to Myles anyway.'

And in his statement to the Bureau of Military History in November 1957, Frank gives us a glimpse into his work as a policeman.

> We had to investigate the larceny of the parish priest's hens. After brief investigation, we found that a servant boy who was attending the parochial house for catechism lessons in preparation for his confirmation, set a hen snare when entering for his lessons and after the PP's lectures on honesty, etc had terminated, the juvenile captured a hen on his way out and sold the bird in the village.

The brothers were significant figures in the republican movement but they didn't really talk about it. Des says of his uncle Sean, 'He didn't talk much about his young days in the IRA. He used to say "The world is your country" – in other words, he was a bit disillusioned.'

But it is from the Bureau of Military History that we learn more about the brothers. In August 1955, Sean signed a witness statement and he describes how he sat the exam to be a clerk in the old GSW railway company and was assigned in June 1914 to Cork. He joined the Volunteers and one of the first raids he was involved in was the seizure of about 100 bicycles from the British military.

A bicycle being a very necessary part of a Volunteer's equipment, orders were issued to capture a quantity of bicycles which had been stored at Woodward's Auction Yard at Copley Street, Cork. About 100 men were mobilised for this operation. After forcing open the gates leading to the yard, each man got orders to select a machine and take it to the place which had been previously selected. I selected what appeared to be a good bicycle and rode away towards the Company HQ, but when I was passing over Brian Boru Bridge, the wheel got stuck in a railway track with the result that I was thrown off the bicycle and, on recovering my feet, I examined the machine to find that the crank was badly bent, rendering the bicycle of no further use for immediate transport. The police having now been alerted, I decided to give the bicycle a watery grave sooner than let it be recaptured, so I dumped it into the bed of the river.

Then in May 1920 and accompanied by his brother Frank, Sean went on a weapon-gathering mission to London, which was to seal his fate romantically.

Our London contacts were Irish girls who were members of the London Cumann na mBan, May Healy and Maire Manning. Both of these girls were then under suspicion, having been arrested and convicted for political activities. The former became my wife on the termination of hostilities.

One particular railway station in Cork proved profitable for the IRA.

> Glanmire Station, Cork, was the scene of many a brilliant raid for arms and was an amazing source of supply. Pistols, revolvers, ammunition, field glasses, other military stores, including complete officers' outfits, were frequently seized. Buses having not yet been introduced into this country, and very few motor cars or lorries being in use, rail travel was the predominant means of transport, and deliveries from trains were effected by means of horse-drawn vehicles. Nearly all trains entering and leaving Glanmire station were packed to capacity ... About 600 men were employed at Glanmire railway station and about 100 of these employees were members of the IRA ...

But the Volunteers had to be creative in sending dispatches.

> The holding up and searching of all trains, at various railway stations, by police and military, had become almost a daily feature from July 1920 to July 1921. They were searching for wanted IRA men, and intelligence communications. Drivers, firemen, guards and ticket checkers were subjected to thorough searches. Every article of their clothing was carefully examined. Therefore, other means had to be devised for outwitting

the searchers. Coffins containing bodies of British soldiers who were killed in action were usually sent home to their relatives in Great Britain for burial. It was the practice to forward the corpses via the Rosslare and Fishguard route, from Cork, loaded in mortuary vans. A ticket checker from Waterford named Peter Millea informed me that, on one occasion, an urgent and important dispatch was being sent from Cork to Fermoy, by the Rosslare train, and the party to whom the dispatch was entrusted, being afraid that it would fall into enemy hands, hit on a novel, though gruesome, idea. He placed it in a coffin which contained the body of a dead soldier. The train was held up and the train crew put through the usual humiliating search, but of course they never opened the coffin of their dead comrade, never dreaming that one of their dead would help the IRA.

Sean was eventually imprisoned in Victoria barracks (now Collins barracks) and he describes his emotions when he was finally released.

It was a glorious sunny evening. The feeling of emotion which came over me when I left the Cage behind was one that I shall never forget. I felt as if I was walking into a new world and fervently thanked God for bringing me safely through the perils and trials which I had endured. I was a free man once more.

Sean got married and had four children, all of whom emigrated. Des says his uncle was 'very disappointed by that. Three of them went to Rhodesia, as it was then.'

The arrival of the Second World War had a severe impact on Ireland, and Ethna remembers being a boarder in the Dominican convent in Eccles Street at the time. 'I would have gone there just before the war started. It was pretty grim, I can tell you. Everything was rationed; we had to have our ration cards. Boarders came back to school with their ration cards; you had to sit at a table yourself and write home for the ration cards as soon as possible so that they would be able to get bread and milk and all the other things.

'Most city streets had big concrete air raid shelters. In Eccles Street there were air raid shelters in the centre of the street. There was a bombing, the North Strand bombing on the 31st of May 1941 in which 28 people were killed. Our air raid shelter was actually the nuns' refectory, which of course was completely out of bounds for us. We were wakened in the middle of the night, told to put on our dressing gowns and bring a pillow and go down to the nuns' refectory, so we were brought down and we had to put our pillow on the table and try and sleep, but of course we were peeking around trying to see what the nuns' refectory was like. It was scary. The nuns' rectory was very plain: tables and chairs, and concrete on the windows. After some time, the bombing was over, and we were brought back to bed.

'Most city streets had big concrete
air raid shelters. In Eccles Street
there were air raid shelters in
the centre of the street.

'I remember we used to have study for half an hour before we started class every morning. We had a study hall at the top of the house and we were there one morning and the next thing a German plane and a British plane flew overhead. The British plane was chasing the German plane and the German plane was making straight for the study-hall window; we were scared out of our wits! Next thing it zoomed up out of the way, and the British plane after it. I think that bombing was probably a mistake: the Germans thought that we were Belfast.'

The British plane was chasing
the German plane and the
German plane was making straight
for the study-hall window.

When Ethna decided to become a nun she entered the Dominican novitiate in Kerdiffstown, County Kildare. She remembers the day of her profession, when 'we were dressed up in the long black dress and the veil, and my brother Leo said to me, "You are not entering the convent until you have smoked at least one cigarette!" In those days everyone smoked, but for some reason I never did, so anyhow, dressed up in all the gear, he brought me out to the back garden, and I smoked my first and last cigarette! So I was in Kerdiffstown for three years, training, and then I came out and went to teach in Scoil Chaitríona in Eccles Street. I taught there for a number of years, and one day I was called by one of my bosses and told that they wanted to send me to UCD to do psychology. I had never heard of psychology – I had to get out a dictionary and look it up! I did psychology and then they said they wanted me to do a master's, which I did, and then they wanted me to do a doctorate, which I did, and then there was a vacancy on the staff in UCD, and they told me to apply for it, which I did, and all of these decisions were made without me! I was in UCD for almost 30 years and it was wonderful, I got to know so many marvellous people who still write to me at Christmas.'

20

Tim Crowley

THE COLLINS CONNECTION

'The thing about it, of course, is that if
the women in Cumann na mBan didn't
feed the IRA and do all they did, the IRA
wouldn't have succeeded in what *they* did.
Only recently have the women been given
credit for their role. They were an integral
part of the success of the revolution.'

In 2010 the Michael Collins Centre opened
in Clonakilty, County Cork and, fittingly, the
proprietor, Tim Crowley, is a relative of the man
himself. Tim has always had a huge interest in history.
'It's a bit of an obsession, and I've a huge interest in
Michael Collins as well and the connection there. We

first opened the centre in 2000 and we started off doing archaeology and general history presentations for visitors, but we were doing Michael Collins talks at night, and they proved to be hugely popular. So we turned it into a Michael Collins museum exclusively.'

Tim aims to bring the story of Michael Collins to life. 'It's not all about facts and dates: you want people to appreciate what it was like to be in the situation. I do a lot of storytelling to kids in school as well. I talk about Michael Collins and I have a rifle in my hands and a bayonet and they love it. Last year we built a replica of an execution yard and there was a post there with a stone. I couldn't get over when we had the first few groups of kids, they all wanted to stand at the post and hold the rifles, and others wanted to put on the blindfolds and see what that was like. I was a bit nervous that it would be a bit morbid and very dark – we go through the protocol of the firing squad and all. But I couldn't get over how the kids reacted to it.'

Tim is proud to have the family connection with Collins. 'I've studied lots of historical figures and that guy seemed to be doing the deed. He was good-looking, charismatic, hugely intelligent, and he was a visionary.' Tim also contemplates how things might have been if Collins had lived. 'I like to think he would have changed politics in Ireland. We can't ever know that. I suppose there are two main parts of Irish history that would have been different. One is the north – in many ways the government abandoned the northern nationals and they were treated like second-class citizens, and we had the Troubles in the 1960s, 1970s, 1980s, 1990s and so on. In 1918 Collins was MP for South Cork, but he was also MP for Armagh – he had a huge interest in the north. I think he would not have abandoned the northern nationals. The other aspect that is often forgotten about Michael Collins is his economic vision; he wasn't just a military man. He never did anything without first asking himself, "Why am I doing that? What am I hoping to achieve?" He had strategy and reason behind everything he did, nothing was done on a whim. There were very few people in our history like that; he stands out.'

He was good-looking, charismatic, hugely intelligent, and he was a visionary.

We chat about the making of the *Michael Collins* film in County Wicklow and the call-out for extras. I tell him I saw busloads of people arrive from all over the country, including many buses from County Cork. 'We're here for Collins,' they'd say, like they were really going to fight for him! And Tim tells me they had a bit of trouble making the movie when Alan Rickman was playing de Valera and making the speeches and there were certain speeches where they wanted the crowd to cheer 'Dev!' and they wouldn't do it!

In 2002 a committee was formed in Clonakilty to erect a statue of Michael Collins in the town but the fundraising was a bit slow. Then Tim was introduced to a Mayo auctioneer who happened to have Liam Neeson's fax number since the film shoot. Liam, of course, played Collins in the movie. The auctioneer suggested getting Neeson to unveil the statue. 'So then the word came back from upstate New York two days later: "I would be honoured and privileged." So of course when the press heard he was coming, it was a totally different situation! We raised over 100,000 euro and we had a week-long festival in Clonakilty and the unveiling of the statue was the last event. Seven and a half thousand people came into the town that evening, the pubs ran out of drink and the restaurants ran out of food. Liam Neeson gave a great speech, and I think that was one of the greatest days of my life. I could live ten lives and I wouldn't have as good a day!'

> Liam Neeson gave a great speech, and I think that was one of the greatest days of my life. I could live ten lives and I wouldn't have as good a day!'

But let's get down to the science bit! Tim's great-grandmother was Marianne Slyne (née McCarthy), a second cousin of Michael Collins' mother, Marianne O'Brien. Marianne Slyne was born in 1856 and had a great sense of her family history, keeping a journal with details of births, marriages and deaths, going back to the decade before she herself was born. The

Marianne Slyne's journal,
recording the death of Michael Collins.

journal ends with the death of Collins and, poignantly, one of the last entries details the deaths of three of her own children.

The Michael Collins Centre has published *Marianne's Journal*, the pages reproduced in his great-grandmother's own copperplate handwriting. Her daughter Elizabeth married Tim's grandfather, Tim Crowley, in 1923. Michael was already dead at that stage and Lizzie was very proud to be related to him.

But the links between the two families were very strong, because Tim's grandfather, Tim Crowley (we'll call him Tim senior), was very active prior to 1916. The Cork brigades were awaiting the arrival of Roger Casement's shipment of arms on the *Aud*, which was intercepted by the Royal Navy on Good Friday 1916 off the coast of Kerry, 'and something like 20,000 Russian rifles failed to land. So there were a lot of marches around Cork and Kerry on Easter Sunday by Volunteers going to different locations to pick up the Casement guns, which of course never arrived. One of those Volunteers was my grandfather, who had marched at dawn to the village of Inchigeelagh on the river Lee, where they were met by Tomás MacCurtain and Terence MacSwiney. The date of that march was the 23rd of April 1916, and of course the following day everything kicked off in Dublin.

'Then on the morning of the 5th of May my grandfather and his brother John were milking the cows on their farm, in the townland just north of Clonakilty. All of a sudden, military lorries and cars pulled up and there was the RIC and Connaught Rangers, and they arrested my grandfather and his brother. They ended up being taken to Cork prison; in fact we have their prison records. From there they were taken by train to Dublin, to Richmond barracks, and they were up there on the 12th of May 1916, and they heard a volley of shots down the street. It was the execution of James Connolly, which was the last execution of the leaders of 1916.

'That evening, according to an account written by Joseph McCarthy from County Wexford, 250 prisoners including my grandfather and his brother were sent to England by ship in very rough conditions. Some of the lads were getting sick, and they were moving around a wooden box – trying to make things a little bit more comfortable for themselves – and the lid slipped off the box and it turned out to be a coffin with a soldier inside who had been killed during the fighting in Dublin two weeks earlier.

The lid slipped off the box and it turned out to be a coffin with a soldier inside who had been killed during the fighting in Dublin two weeks earlier.

'The prisoners were taken to Wakefield prison in Yorkshire and then moved to Frongach in Wales, which afterwards became known as the "University of Revolution". Joseph McCarthy mentions that he was kept in lock number 3, with prisoners he named out, including Richard Mulcahy, Michael Collins and the Crowley brothers from Clonakilty. So we know that my grandfather and my granduncle were in the same lock as Michael Collins. My grandfather and granduncle were released in July, after spending about two months in prison.

'My grandfather was born in 1877, so he was actually in his early forties during the War of Independence, and therefore too old to go on with Michael Collins and all that. Because of his age he wasn't part of the ambushes, but he was part of the support network. His house became the local battalion headquarters for the IRA. Last year we discovered two Cumann na mBan pension files for two of my grandaunts, who were his sisters, Ellen and Mary Crowley. We found them in the Irish Military Archives. The sisters were talking about supplying about 50 or 60 méals a week to the IRA, giving them beds, looking after their weapons; there was a typewriter in the house and even court martials were held there. The thing about it, of course, is that if the women in Cumann na mBan didn't feed the IRA and do all they did, the IRA wouldn't have succeeded in what *they* did. Only recently have the women been given credit for their role. They were an integral part of the success of the revolution.

'The big bombshell for me was that my grandfather was a mad Fine Gael man, and his brother John was a mad Fine Gael man, but the two sisters in their accounts said that they took the anti-treaty side in the Civil War! So I can't figure out what the dynamic was in that house at that time. It was a big shock to me.

'My grandfather's family were farmers and they were carrying on their normal business, but genuinely during that time they were uneasy because the door could be burst in at three o'clock in the morning and the Black and Tans would storm in. My great-grandfather was John Crowley and we have an account from 1916 of the police storming into his bedroom and he tried to hit them with the stick beside the bed! They were searching under the bed for guns.'

My great-grandfather was John Crowley
and we have an account from 1916 of
the police storming into his bedroom
and he tried to hit them with the
stick beside the bed! They were
searching under the bed for guns.

Tim says his own father, Dan, was 'a mad GAA man! He developed an interest in history very late in life. He died in 2017 – he was almost 90. A few years before that he had an operation on his ankle; he had been a farmer all his life and he was fed up with spending a lot of time indoors with his leg up. So I got on to him and encouraged him to write his memoir, and that's the third book we published in the family. It was mainly the story of a farmer. It's called *My Time in My Place*.' In the book, Dan talks about his mother, Elizabeth Slyne, who lived to the ripe old age of 93 and who was very skilled at raising poultry, and she often had the best turkeys in the Christmas sale at Inchybridge creamery. She died in 1982 and is buried with her husband, who died in 1958. 'He died in the western bedroom upstairs,' Tim tells me, 'and because his coffin wouldn't fit down the stairs, it was lowered from the southern window on two planks to the ground.'

> He died in the western bedroom
> upstairs and because his coffin
> wouldn't fit down the stairs,
> it was lowered from the southern
> window on two planks to the ground.

Tim's parents, Dan Crowley and Julia O'Leary,
were married on 13 June 1961. Julia came from
the local mill. 'My mother's older brother was Pat
O'Leary; he never married. He was a miller, a farmer
and a natural historian. He would come up to our
house every Friday night and he would light the pipe
and he would tell stories. My brothers would often
slip upstairs but I was sitting glued to every word
that came out of his mouth. He was born during the
War of Independence; he was only a year old during
the war, but he retained so many of the stories from
around here of what happened.

'There was one other interesting character on my
mother's side. His name was Tim Hurley; he was
my mother's granduncle. In 1886 he had the mill
that my mother was born in rented from a landlord
called Martin Bennett. He couldn't pay rent to the
landlord that year, there was a bit of a recession in
the milling industry, and Bennett arranged to evict
Tim and his family from the mill. This story was
illustrated by a sketch artist who actually sketched
the mill ... but it was an example of a failed eviction
because they came with the bailiffs and the police
with a battering ram and so on, and the mill was
about six storeys in height. When the bailiffs and
the police were leaving Clonakilty, some local
people started sounding the church bells, and up
on the hill people were blowing cow horns, to alert

the locality that the eviction team was on the way. Fifteen hundred spectators came out to see what was happening.

'They tried to burst in the doors and the windows with a battering ram, but Tim had cut away the stairs in the door of the mill – and he and some of the neighbours had taken refuge up under the roof of the upper storey – the mill was about six storeys in height – so they couldn't get near them! And from their vantage point they started throwing down bits of bricks and boiling water and all ... same idea as a round tower. In the end the police lined up in the yard as a firing squad and they were going to start firing at the mill, but the local priest stopped them.

'There was one woman from Clonakilty, her name was O'Leary as well, she was a bit of an entrepreneur, because she came out from the town with a big basket of biscuits and she started selling them to the spectators. And so Tim shouted over, "Come over here, Mary, and we'll buy some of your biscuits!" So she went over and they dropped down a basket on a rope, and they were just about to put the biscuits into the basket when the police came along and took it away. Then Tim came out of the mill with two big baskets of loaves and he said, "We can hold on here for two weeks!" and there was a big cheer from the crowd.

Dan Crowley, holding a page from *Marianne's Journal* detailing his mother's birth in 1889.

'My mother's father was Thomas O'Leary. He was a local story-teller, and I have a collection of his tales as well. He used to tell a story that he shot a salmon with a ramrod musket in the river, but that he had run out of bullets, so instead he used the seeds of a hawthorn tree. He shot the salmon and the salmon escaped, and about 12 months later he was back on the same stretch of riverbank again and he saw this little tree growing on top of the water and he couldn't figure out what it was. He went over and had a closer look and wasn't it growing out of the back of the fish that he had shot with the hawthorn seed!'

And does Tim believe that story?

'Definitely!'

21

Mary Wallace

A PENNY WORTH
OF SWEETS

'If you were lucky enough, you
lived. Going to see a doctor would be
the last thing you'd do. That's the
way it was in those days.'

'I grew up in a 300-year-old house filled with stories and visiting storytellers, but no other family member or relatives could possibly rival in my young ears my aunt Mary Wallace or uncle John, nor my father, who alone told his stories in song.'

I'm chatting with Richard O'Farrell, now the keeper of his family history, which has been traced all the way back to the Tribes of Kilkenny of the 1400s. In 1985, a very special thing happened: Richard's aunt Mary agreed to a recorded interview, along with her nephew, Fr Pat O'Farrell. Richard carried out the recording.

'On my regular visits to aunt Mary,' Richard tells me, 'who was residing with her daughter Bríd Callinan, she was always recalling people and events from years long past, so I decided to bring my ghetto-blaster and tape recorder and ask her a few questions. She was 85 at the time.'

First, she described where she lived.

Our lane used to be the roadway along which every funeral passed from Kilcurl to Callan. My grandfather, James Dalton, used to tell of how our house was reversed, the front becoming the back, to provide a right-of-way when the farm was split in two between ancestors of the O'Farrells and the O'Keeffes of today. My grandfather used to tell of how the thatched roof fell in in 1806, when he was 18 years old, after a big storm and a heavy fall of snow. It was an old house then, by far the oldest one there, and his father and grandfather lived all their lives there too. It was an unusual house, built in days before cement and mortar, a two-storey thatched and hipped house.

Mary had been born on the family farm in Kilcurl, Knocktopher, County Kilkenny on 28 January

1901 to parents John O'Farrell (1866–1918) and Brigid Ryan (1867–1945). She was the third eldest in a family of nine children. In her early life, Mary was faced with much tragedy – her aunt, Mary Ann Hartley of Busherstown, her father, John, and her sister, Sr Kathleen, aged 20, all died in 1918 of the so-called 'big flu'. Then her younger brother James died in 1925, aged 19, of appendicitis complications; her newborn sister Ellen died of bronchitis in 1912 when just five days old; and her little sister Alice died after an illness in 1922, aged 9. On 11 August 1926 Mary married William Wallace (1882–1967) of Stonecarthy, Stoneyford and they had a family of six children, four boys and two girls – the late Jim, then Jack, Bob, Rev. Monsignor Paddy, Anna (Sr Pauline) and Bríd Callinan.

> Her aunt, Mary Ann Hartley of
> Busherstown, her father, John, and
> her sister, Sr Kathleen, aged 20, all died
> in 1918 of the so-called 'big flu'.

Aunt Mary was the elder sister of Richard's father, also Richard (Dick), a well-known Kilkenny farmer and a member of Ballyhale Village Creamery Co-operative. It amalgamated with over 30 other Kilkenny village creamery co-ops in 1967 to collectively give birth to the ground-breaking Avonmore Co-operative and over time it grew exponentially to become Glanbia Plc. But Dick was best known locally as the Carlow sugar beet factory agent for south Kilkenny, until his retirement in 1969, after 33 years.

'Her youngest brother, Sean (John) O'Farrell,' Richard tells me, 'was a Kilkenny All-Ireland hurler. He became the second of only three managing directors of the National Ploughing Association

Wedding of Mary Wallace's grandparents,
2 August 1893. Left-right: Catherine Tracey O'Farrell,
Fr Thomas Hartley, the bride's brother John O'Farrell,
Fr James O'Farrell, the bride Mary Ann O'Farrell
and the groom James Hartley.

(NPA) and National Ploughing Championships (NPC), from 1958 to 1972.

'Aunt Mary often talked about a third brother too, my uncle Fr Pat O'Farrell (1900–56), whom I remember as a small kid. She usually spoke of him in reverent tones as the Gaelic scholar that brought back the 'O' into our family name. Fr Pat received a licentiate of sacred theology degree from Alberinum, University of Fribourg, Switzerland in 1927.

'Woodstock House was the notorious local HQ for the Black and Tans in Kilkenny. There were many stories of the Tans arriving at farm houses with "reliable" information to hand, but on being denied confirmation of same, helping themselves to the "hospitality" of the owners, essentially stealing their food and drink. This was at a time when people had barely enough to survive. Mary's husband William was imprisoned at Woodstock during the 1920–2 period.'

> There were many stories of the Tans arriving at farm houses with 'reliable' information to hand, but on being denied confirmation of same, helping themselves to the 'hospitality' of the owners, essentially stealing their food and drink. This was at a time when people had barely enough to survive.

Richard tells the story of how his own father, Dick, overheard of the planned ambush of a neighbour one day and rode on his bicycle for 14 miles to warn him to come back by another road. The neighbour survived, and his family never forgot the deed. 'That neighbour became like a mentor to me as a kid as I readily "volunteered" to help him thin his beloved vegetable quarter-acre or maintain in high order his hedges on our lane. Our families remain especially close to this day.'

But, back to Mary's interview. She had a great memory and went right back to her own childhood to describe the scarcity of money.

When did we see it ... money? I'll give you an instance of that. Pat and Katie were the oldest in my family, and they were sick with measles, I think. So they coaxed Dick and me [their siblings] to go to school; the road was lonely so they'd give us a penny between us. That's the way you saw money! And we were so proud of that penny that I went into Kitty Darcy's little shop and changed the penny into two halfpennies and I gave Dick his halfpenny and I kept mine. And during the day I was admiring the halfpenny, thinking about what I'd buy, mostly to bring home; if you bought a penny worth of sweets, you brought most of them to the ones at home. But didn't the halfpenny slip out of my hand and there was a hole in the floor of the classroom and it went into it. So Dick had a halfpenny while I was left heartbroken. That's how plentiful money was in those days!

Financially, it was a tough time for widows.

There was the poor relief of a half-crown per week for the widow (notably equal to the amount expected in the offerings to the priest at Sunday mass) with a few pence added per child a week. Sure it was only a starvation diet. Then when the old age pension came in in 1909, it was 5 shillings a week. I was about 10 years at the time but I can remember everyone was running for their birth certificate. People who wouldn't admit they were 70 before were then sure to be over 70!

Successful single claimants over the age of 70 were paid five shillings a week, while couples, where the husband was aged over 70, got seven shillings and sixpence per week. At that time a workman earned five to six shillings a week and if he was a ploughman he got six shillings a week and his food.

But despite the lack of money in rural Ireland, Mary said people were generous towards the church.

That was known as the parish priest's quest in the 1950s.

> People would put a half-crown in the collection box offerings at mass for the priest or curate; you didn't offer him less. I think people were more generous in their own way in those days with the little they did have than people are today. Another thing that was very common, and it's gone: as a farming people, you brought a load of turnips to the priest or curate, or a cow or a couple of calves maybe, or gave him a bag of oats and a turkey or a pair of chickens at Christmas. People were generous, in kind.

As a farming people, you brought a load
of turnips to the priest or curate, or a cow
or a couple of calves maybe, or give him
a bag of oats and a turkey or a pair of
chickens at Christmas.

Mary also remembered her first new dress.

> I got a new dress for my confirmation, I was 11 years old. It was a beautiful white dress, and I loved it. I only got to wear it three times, though – once on the day of my confirmation, once for

the procession in Knocktopher, and once when I was brought to see my aunt Alice (Sr Mary Alacoque) Ryan in Thomastown convent. Then it was put back in the box to keep it for my younger sister, Statia. I cried at the thoughts of only getting to wear it three times. Statia said she cried her eyes out because they lent it out to Lisa Barden who was confirmed two days before her, before she got to wear it herself. People used to get a loan of a dress; that's the way people lived.

New shoes weren't very plentiful when Mary was a child.

Sure we went barefoot in summertime. We didn't get a shoe at all. And the roads weren't like they are now – there were plenty of loose stones on them. And the boys were devils: they'd put stones in the dust, the dust used to be two inches high on the roads, so you'd hit your toe off them. So you went barefoot, and then, come the fall, mother and father would harness up, and in the morning we'd start out for Kilkenny. Everyone was measured up the night before for the new pair of shoes or boots. I remember being overjoyed for my confirmation as I got a new pair of shoes with bows on them.

Sure we went barefoot in summertime.
We didn't get a shoe at all. And the roads
weren't like they are now – there were
plenty of loose stones on them.

There wasn't much travel either. Mary said her first time away from the homeplace was for a funeral.

It was my first visit up to Kilkenny, 13 miles away, to meet a funeral heading for burial in Ballyhale. Then to a dentist, my first visit, it was down to Waterford, aged 16 or 17. There were no school inspections then; they did not start until I was married and my kids hardy enough to go there.

And as for visiting the doctor?

If you were lucky enough, you lived. Going to see a doctor would be the last thing you'd do. That's the way it was in those days.

And Mary recalled her older sister Katie's death at 20 years of age, in the so-called 'Spanish flu' of 1918.

Katie was a nun in the Mercy convent, New Ross. Her religious name was Sr Kieran and the family received two telegrams at the same time from Sr Vincent, the reverend mother. The first, sent on the morning of Katie's death, said, 'Sr Kieran bad again, pray'. Then she sent a second telegram an hour later to say Sr Kieran had died. Both telegrams were wired an hour apart, but were only delivered at 4 p.m. Telegrams in those days were given by the local post office to whoever was passing by your place. Don't say they were the good old times; they weren't. I wouldn't go back to them.

These were the days when horse and trap were the best mode of transport available, and New Ross was 40 miles away.

Mary Wallace's father, John O'Farrell,
and his two eldest children,
Kathleen (Sr Kieran) and Patrick (Fr Pat).

> Don't say they were the good old times;
> they weren't. I wouldn't go back to them.

'There is a strong family tradition of nuns and priests that runs through my family for generations right up to this day,' Richard tells me. 'My eldest sister, Sr Bríd [Attracta] is a retired school principal of the Mercy convent, Carrick-on-Suir. My younger sister, the late Sr Maura, was a Mercy nun too and also a nurse, who died in 2013 after a lengthy illness aged 67.'

But there was a calendar of big events in Knocktopher.

> The 16th of July was a great day – you were preparing for that for weeks. There would be five or six stands outside the chapel gate. We would get a full tumbler of ripe gooseberries for a penny and would get the brown Peggy's leg bar for a halfpenny. We always got twopence to spend that day. You'd buy a lot for that twopence. But that was only once a year. About four of us children would go, and we'd be in the procession too.

The liturgical feast of Our Lady of Mount Carmel was celebrated on 16 July each year. The Carmelites were then in Knocktopher.

Then there'd be the sports in Knocktopher, New-market and Croan. It would be great, with bicycle riding. Gerry Lennon of Knocktopher used to win all the races. Sure, you made your own amusements: cricket was popular but we played it our own way, as kids, not the way it should be played; skittles, funny enough, there was a game of skittles in every house; hurling came in later. The beginning of hurling in our house was my brother John – he was in St Kieran's College in the 1920s, he had the knack, and he was a good hurler. They played it in the *cruachdene* [haggard field] with the Powers of Ballybooden. That's my remembrance of it.

And in 1985 Mary had this advice:

They were hard times and people had to live hard. The 1914–18 war was the first bit of prosperity, to the smaller farmer anyway, because he began to get better prices for his cattle and pigs that gave him a little more independence. Before that, they were hard times. But back then people were agreeable to live in the hard times; they're not now. They must have spending money now.

Terence FitzPatrick

ONE OF 200,000 IRISHMEN

'To my own darling son from his
loving Daddy who is far away.'

Dubliner Terence FitzPatrick became one of the 'old contemptibles', the British soldiers who went to northern France in 1914 in order to support the French. More than 200,000 Irishmen joined up and fought in the British army in the First World War and 35,000 lost their lives. Many joined for economic reasons. However, those at home who took the opportunity, against the background of the war, to launch an armed rebellion in the quest for an independent Irish republic were not happy to see Irishmen fighting overseas on the British side.

In his witness statement to the Bureau of Military History, Sean Healy, whose story appears elsewhere in this book, wrote:

> After the Easter Week Rising there was a big falling off in the number of Irishmen who volunteered for war service in the English army and the British authorities now resorted to economic pressure in every possible direction using the vilest propaganda to try and lure young men into their army. Employers were directed to guarantee re-employment to any of their employees who volunteered for active service, on being discharged, and, in some cases, half pay was allowed by the firms to volunteers, and those who did not join the British forces were in several cases threatened with dire consequences after the war was over. 'Rolls of Honour' were drawn up by some of the larger concerns such as railway companies and banks giving details of those who had gone to serve His Majesty, the King of England.

The British authorities now resorted to economic pressure in every possible direction using the vilest propaganda to try and lure young men into their army.

In 1918 there was an attempt to introduce conscription in Ireland, which angered a lot of people but which also had the effect of encouraging young men to join the Volunteers instead of the British army. Sean Healy:

> In the year 1918 the World War was at its height when the British passed a conscription Act to compel Irishmen to join the British army. This Act was the means of greatly strengthening our ranks, as large numbers of young men then joined the Irish Volunteers in preference to the British forces, but the majority of what we termed 'conscripts' left the organisation again when the danger passed over. However, a good number remained faithful to the end.

Terence FitzPatrick joined the army in 1914 and was a territorial soldier in the army service corps, where

Terence and his wife, May.

his profession was listed as 'machine man'. His company was attached to the 5th infantry division, which was based in The Curragh at the outset of hostilities. This was a horse-based unit. Terence arrived in France in mid-August 1914, a regular soldier with just a couple of months' service. His first post was to northern France but he was probably posted to Italy in late 1917, before returning to the western front in mid-1918.

While he was away, his wife, May Hackett, gave birth to their first child, Jack. The couple exchanged postcards; these were official army postcards that included propaganda messages on the front, and some of them were specifically designed for couples to stay in touch.

One such card sent by Terence to his newly born son, Jack, showed a young boy with a rifle and was titled 'The Dream'. On the back he wrote:

To my own darling son from his loving Daddy who is far away.

May responded with a photo of the child, dated 17 March 1918:

To my own dearest husband,
From May & Jackie with all our love.
XXXXX

For one of the Christmases they were separated, May sent another card:

> *Wishing my own dearest husband a very happy Xmas. Dearest Terry write me a long letter soon and cheer up old sport, as there is better days coming. Please God. Everyone at home sends their best love to you they also wish you a very happy Xmas. Heaps of love and kisses from your very lonely and devoted wife. May. Write soon. XXXXXXX*

The front of the wartime postcard that May sent to Terence at Christmas when he was fighting in France.

Terence was allowed home to visit in mid-1918, and the following February their second son, Terence Jnr, was born. The couple went on to have five sons – Jack, Terry, Des, Gerry and Brendan – and three daughters: Eileen, Frances and Kathleen. Brendan, the youngest, born in 1929, is the sole survivor.

Brendan remembers grow-ing up on Killeen Road in Rathmines and all the neighbours' children playing together on the road. There were 15 years between Jack and Brendan. 'When I was a kid he was working. He worked in the ESB like the rest of them. I was the only one who didn't go into the ESB. I served my time as a tradesman. My brother Gerry joined the RAF but everyone just accepted it – there was no reaction to him joining.'

Brendan met the love of his life, Eileen, in the Crystal Ballroom in Dublin. 'We started dating in 1962. We were engaged for about four years and then we got married.' The couple had two children but sadly Eileen passed in 1997. Brendan still misses her, but says, 'I had a very happy life. I'm very happy with how things went for me.'

Brendan recalls that his father was an only child but his mother had two sisters and two brothers. One of those brothers, Christy Hackett, served his apprenticeship as a baker with the Jewish Bretzel bakery on Lennox Street in Dublin. The Bretzel

Terence meets his two-year-old son, Jack, for the first time.

opened in 1870 and had always been run by Jewish families. However, when the time came for the then owners, the Stein family, to retire, he sold the business to Christy. Christy was a Catholic but he continued the Jewish tradition, with the rabbi attending each morning to confirm that everything was done in the proper kosher manner. In 2000 the Hacketts sold the bakery to William Despard, who maintains the bakery's kosher status.

Acknowledgements

This book was mainly written through the magic of the telephone and Zoom calls! Covid put a stop to my usual jaunts around the country, drinking tea and chatting and making new friends. I really want to thank everyone I interviewed for their kindness and patience in putting up with the long phone calls, the repeat calls, the check-up calls and the quest for family photographs from long ago.

Thank you to those who facilitated the interviews, especially Elaine FitzPatrick-English and Niall Cox, and thanks to Ruth McCormack who has a great ear for recorded interviews!

Many thanks to John Goodman, Great War historian, for the research on my grandfather, Terence FitzPatrick (Chapter 22). I am also grateful to the Bureau of Military History, Military Archives for permission to use the extracts from the witness statements of Sean Healy (WS1479, File S.2703); Francis Healy (WS1694, File S.3017) and Sean O'Keeffe (WS1261, File S.2576).

Thank you to the Kavanagh family for permission to use the photographs for Chapter 4 (Edward Kavanagh) from the archives of Paul Kavanagh, photographer. Thanks also to Tim Collins of the

Michael Collins Centre in Clonakilty, Co Cork for permission to reproduce the photographs from *Marianne's Diary*, published by the centre.

Writing a book needs the support of family and friends and I have been very lucky in both regards! My lovely husband, Brian, cast his eye over the drafts, and my children – Brian, Emily, Eoin, Maeve and Aengus – remembered to ask me how it was going!

My wonderful friends got late night updates and my pal, Deirdre Purcell, gifted me her enthusiasm and inspiration along the way. Thank you!

My dogs, Ben and Sammy, also played their part, keeping me company during those long nights when inspiration flowed.

But, of course, there would be no book without the publishers, the wonderful people at Hachette Books Ireland. Firstly, my publisher and editor, Ciara Considine, whose encouragement kept us going during Covid and who spotted solutions before the problems were apparent – thank you. Sincere thanks also to all the team at Hachette, including copy-editor Aonghus Meaney, typesetter Claire Rourke, proofreader Emma Dunne and publicity director Elaine Egan.

I really loved writing this book, engaging with people whose parents and grandparents lived remarkable lives and whose contribution to the Ireland we have today may not have been documented until now. I take great pleasure in telling their stories so that you, the reader, can relive this remarkable period in our history, this insight into a world of idealism, suffering, violence, joy and independence.